Urban Underground Space
Design in China

Urban Underground Space Design in China

Vernacular and Modern Practice

GIDEON S. GOLANY

DELAWARE

Newark: University of Delaware Press
London and Toronto: Associated University
Presses

Associated University Presses
440 Forsgate Drive
Cranbury, NJ 08512

Associated University Presses
25 Sicilian Avenue
London WC1A 2QH, England

Associated University Presses
P.O. Box 488, Port Credit
Mississauga, Ontario
Canada L5G 4M2

The paper used in this publication meets the requirements of the American National Standard for Permanence of Paper for Printed Library Materials Z39.48-1984.

Library of Congress Cataloging-in-Publication Data

Golany, Gideon.
  Urban underground space design in China.

  Bibliography: p.
  Includes index.
  1. Underground architecture—China. 2. Vernacular architecture—China. I. Title.
NA2542.7.G65 1989   720   87-40708
ISBN 0-87413-345-9 (alk. paper)

PRINTED IN THE UNITED STATES OF AMERICA

Dedicated to my old friends
Debora and Ehud Krongrad,
Ruth and Adi Amorai,
their children and
grandchildren.

Contents

Figures

Preface

The prime theme of this book is to introduce to the reader both the accomplishment of the vernacular and the evaluation of modern, non-residential, below-ground space facilities in China. This book is the result of a one-year field survey (1984–85) throughout China and the accumulation of data for a number of years before the field survey. The seeds of a below-ground research project were planted during my youth, which was spent in a desert region in a semi-below-ground house, and also during the late 1940s, when I was a founder and member of the kibbutz settlement of Bea'ri, in the arid zone of southern Israel. The ultimate design of this volume inevitably began there, when I dug into the loess soil of the kibbutz to build shelters and trenches for defense, and when I observed closely nomads of the region storing their food for many seasons in well-articulated below-ground storage pits. It is only recently that I have been able to transfer this vision into a reality through the Chinese and other case studies.

China, more than any other nation in the world, has been using below-ground space continuously since before 2000 B.C. The Chinese have gained a wealth of experience that can be included in modern design practices, as has been noted in this study. In any case, since the recent energy crises in the West, there has been a steady increase of international interest in sophisticated methods of development of below-ground space. This new movement has taken place primarily in industrialized countries such as the United States, Japan, Sweden, Russia, and Canada. The

need for civil defense brought the Chinese government to accelerate the large-scale development of below-ground space in the 1960s, especially in the cities of Beijing, where a very high percentage of space usage is below ground at the present time, and Shanghai. These immense spaces are now used as hotels, shopping centers, assembly halls, theaters, dance halls, food storage areas, public gathering places, and for many other types of uses.

The field survey in China was designed to collect comprehensive data on the subject; to visit a large number of sites; to interview many persons involved in the usage, preservation, or design of below-ground space; to photograph, map, and survey selected sites, and last, to measure dry- and wet-bulb temperatures. The latter was done diurnally every hour for twenty-four hours in both the winter (1984) and the summer (1985), for purposes of comparative analysis. In any thermal performance study, research of sites having different functions is an essential tool for analysis. Here it has been treated fully. Much of this research was conducted in the city of Shanghai, taking as case studies five below-ground structures: a workers' hospital, a furniture exhibition hall, a large department store, a workers' club, and a restaurant.

There is a lack of information in English on the Chinese past and present experience in the usage of below-ground space. In addition to the field survey, we needed to translate from Chinese into English chapters of books, a large number of articles, and much of the gathered data.

The procreation of this book is therefore a joint effort of many of my Chinese and American friends and students, to whom I owe much thanks and appreciation. I am grateful to the American National Academy of Sciences for a grant to cover the period of my research in China and to Tongji University in Shanghai for facilitating my itinerary and assisting in the project. I owe thanks to Dr. Charles Hosler, vice-president for research of the Pennsylvania State University, and to Dr. James Moeser, dean of the College of Arts and Architecture for their decisive support. I am grateful to my former department head, Professor Raniero Corbelletti, who encouraged me during the preparation of this manuscript and offered advice when reviewing the drawings; and to the Laboratory for Environmental Design and Planning of the College of Arts and Architecture. I am also grateful to former associate dean for research and graduate programs, Ms. Eliza Pennypacker, who was most helpful. I am thankful for all of their support. I am also indebted to Mr. Loukas Kalisperis, who prepared all the graphs through our ACL-COM-CAD computer laboratory, to my assistants Ms. Wu Hua, Deng Dong, Wang Jianzhong, and Ms. Yang Xiaohui, who helped prepare the final drafting of the drawings. Professor Shirley Wood, Ms. Yu Li Juan, Dr. Y. S. Lee, and Mr. Luke Leung were of great help in translating texts from Chinese into English, and I thank them for their dedication. I am also grateful to Mrs. Linda Gummo for the careful typing of the text; last, to Mrs. Grace Perez, for her perseverance and attention to detail while working on this volume from its early stages, my great appreciation and thanks. Without them all this volume would not have been possible.

Acknowledgments

I would like to thank those who helped me in the realization of this research, both before and during my stay in China:

National Academy of Sciences, and especially Mr. Robert Geyer, director of the National Program for Advanced Study and Research in China of the Committee on Scholarly Communication with the People's Republic of China, Washington, D.C., and his program assistant, Mr. Jeff Filcik.

The staff of the Chinese Ministry of Metallurgical Industry, Beijing, who sponsored my research project during my stay in China. A large number of their key personnel facilitated every detail of my research plans; without their perceptive help this research could not have been realized. Among them are Mr. Wang Zu-Cheng, director of the education department; Mr. Li Wenjian, vice director of the education department; Mr. Yang Song-Tao, engineer, foreign affairs department; Mr. Li Fu-Qin, translator, division of higher education.

Most helpful were the many staff members of the American Embassy in Beijing: Dr. Jack L. Gosnell, counselor for science and technology, and his assistants, Mr. Christopher J. Marut and Mr. Douglas B. McNeal; the first secretary and cultural affairs officer, Dr. Karl F. Olsson; and Mr. Lynn H. Noah, counselor for press and cultural affairs.

The Architectural Society of China, which, along with the Ministry of Metallurgical Industry, was effective in managing my itinerary. Among the many are architect Ren Zhenying, head of the investigation group on the Chinese cave dwellings; Mr. Huang Sin-Fan, director of the academic affairs divison; Mr. Gong Deshun, former secretary of the ASC; Ms. Xi Jingda, director of the department of foreign affairs; Mr. Jin Oubu and Mr. Zeng Jian of the ASC; and Professor Chen Zhanxiang of the China Academy of Urban Planning and Design.

Also the many persons from Xian Institute of Metallurgy and Construction Engineering: President and Professor Zhao Hongzuo; Mr. Zhang Guang and Mr. Zhang Peixul of the department of foreign affairs; members of the department of architecture, Professor Guang Shi-Kui, head, and Professors Zhang Si-Zan, Xia Yun, my assistant Mr. Qiao Zhen, and, last but not least, my friend Professor Hou Ji Yao, who was most helpful with advice on arranging my research plan.

The large number of persons at Tongji University in Shanghai, among them: Professor Hou Xue Yuan, head of the department of geotechnical engineering and my assistants during additional field research in Shanghai, Mr. Su Yu and Mr. Peng Fristo.

Others at Beijing University of Iron and Steel Technology: President and Professor Wang Run; Professor Yu Zong-sen, dean of the faculty of physical chemistry; Professor Huang Wu-Di, provost and director of our newly initiated interdisciplinary graduate program on environmental design; Professor Qiao Duan; and Mr. Dali Yang and Mr. Zhao Yong-Lu, interpreters.

In Shanxi Province: Architect Zuo Guo Bao of the Architectural Scientific Academy of Shanxi and Mr. Lin Yi Shan, director of the Institute of Building Science; Mr. Li Minhong and Mr. Qiao Shuong Wong, both of Taiyuan City Construction Committee; Mr. Jia Kuen Nan of the Architectural Society of Linfen region; and Mr. Lian Peng, interpreter with the foreign affairs office of Linfen region.

In Shaanxi Province: Mr. Wang Zheng Ji, head of Fen Hue team, Liquan county, Mr. Wang Yang Chang, leader at the foreign affairs division, and Mr. Li Jian Qien, architect; from Yan'an city Mr. Wei Tan King, construction engineer of Yan'an region, and Mr. Zhang Zong Qiang of the foreign affairs office.

In Gansu Province: Mr. Ren Zhenying, chief architect of Lanzhou City, and Mr. Nan Ying Jing, translator and engineer of Lanzhou City; Mr. Jing of the Qingyang regional government; Mr. Wang Jiu Ru of the Architectural Society of Qingyang region and head of the office of urban and rural construction and environmental protection.

In Henan Province; Professor Shirley Wood, dean of the foreign language department and honorary director of graduate studies, Henan University, Kaifeng, was most helpful, as was artist Wang Jianzhong of Henan University, who assisted me greatly before and during my stay in China; in Zhengzhou city, architect Lee Lian Shing, Architectural Society of Henan, Mr. Chow Pei Nan of the Architectural Academy of Zhengzhou City; in Gong Xian county, Ms. Zhong Chueng Rueng and Mr. Lee Jin Lu, engineers with the department of construction; and in Luoyang city, Mr. Lee Chuan Zhe and Mr. Wang An Min of the Architectural Society of Luoyang region.

And finally at Tsinghua University, Beijing: Professor Li Daozeng, dean of the department of architecture, and Professors Cai Junfu and Wu Huanjia, both of the department of architecture.

To all my thanks and deep appreciation for their perceptive help and warm hospitality.

Introduction

The use of subterranean space in China has a history of more than four thousand years. Such below-ground space usage has occurred primarily in the region of loess soil (yellow soil), which spreads over the five provinces of Shaanxi, Shanxi, Henan, Ningxia, and Gansu. This 1,000 kilometer-wide strip stretches from the arid zone of the far northwest, eastward to central China for more than 2,500 kilometers. In this region the usage has been primarily, but not exclusively, for dwellings; other common vernacular uses of below-ground space were for food storage and for the tombs of kings and nobles. Approximately 35 to 40 million people live today in cave dwellings in this zone. Recently the use of subterranean space has expanded beyond this zone to other places in China to include a variety of structures, such as restaurants, shopping centers, assembly halls, hospitals, theaters, and manufacturing plants. During the 1960s, due to the political tension between China and the U.S.S.R., construction of below-ground space in major cities was highly accelerated and large underground spaces designated for civil defense were built. Today most of these spaces are used as hotels, shopping centers, and so on, with the major conversion of such space occurring in the cities of Beijing and Shanghai (fig. 1).

The Chinese philosophy of below-ground space usage has coincided with and also differed from the basic concept prevailing in most other places of the world where large-scale development of subterranean dwellings has taken place, such as in southern Tunisia (Matmata Plateau), central Turkey (Cappadocia), southern Italy (Trulli), and some locations in Spain. In those places a prime motivation was the need to cope with a harsh, dry, hot climate. In general, the soil provides a one-season time lag by allowing the summer heat to penetrate the soil to a depth of 10 meters, thus warming the below-ground space in the winter. Cool summers below ground result from the penetration of the previous winter's cold. In the case of China, most of the cave dwellers enjoy these great climatic advantages, especially those who live in arid and semi-arid Gansu, Shanxi, Shaanxi, and most of Henan provinces. The Chinese development of subterranean space was also motivated by other factors such as the need to save agricultural land; the availability of loess soil, making digging relatively easy; the fact that such construction is inexpensive and uses simple tools; and the economy that results when wasteland (such as a cliffside) can be utilized. In the past the basic reasons for using below-ground space primarily involved saving energy; food storage; survival; affordability; use of low technology; and economy of building materials. In modern times the prime motivations have been the need to preserve agricultural civil defense; the advantage of dual land usage in congested urban centers; energy savings; and economy.

Modern below-ground facilities exist in large numbers today throughout China. Many are located within urban centers outside the loess soil zone of the north, especially in Chongqing, Sichuan Province. In this city we found refriger-

Fig. 1. Below-ground tourist shop, originally part of the underground shelter designated for civil defense.

ated meat- and vegetable-storage facilities, a tea-house, the Watch and Clock Company, and the manufacturing plant of the Sichuan Ship Repair Yard, as well as natural ventilation systems for cooling the above-ground Wide-Screen Cinema and the Chongqing Cigarette Factory. Subterranean tunnels and conference rooms exist in Chongqing, Beijing, Shanghai, and many other cities, and there is a theater and dance hall in Hangzhou, Zhejiang province. The famous Resistance College and the Lushun Art College in Yan'an city, Shaanxi Province, also utilize below-ground structures as school buildings, as does Yan'an University, which increasingly uses subterranean classrooms and dormitories. The Middle School of Fenghuo Brigade in Liquan County, Shaanxi Province, was built in 1979 on the terraced slope of a hill; however, it has now been abandoned because of poor design and construction (fig. 2). Tourist hotels and restaurants with adobe vaults are being built in Lanzhou city, Gansu; in Yan'an city, Shaanxi; in Turpan city, Xinjiang; and in other cities. There

are many warehouses and storage structures, cellars for vegetables, potatoes, fruit, wine, ice, water, and so forth, in a large number of cave dwellings of the loess soil zone; there are also underground facilities containing huge quantities of grain. Their construction cost is half that of those facilities above ground. They have stable temperature and humidity, less oxygen, and are free from rats, birds, and worms. There are many public and utility structures, tombs, and mausoleums scattered throughout China, as well as garages and storage places for agricultural machinery in cliffside caves.[1]

Devoting below-ground space in China to non-residential use was given much support in the 1960s when Chairman Mao instituted the policy of digging tunnels for civil defense, with local governments, including communes and factories, being given the initiative. Shortly thereafter the use of below-ground space was institutionalized on a large scale, especially in large cities such as Shanghai and Beijing. In most cases the secondary use of these spaces has evolved

Fig. 2. Below-ground cliffside classrooms of a school in Liquan County, Shaanxi Province.

from a desire to make efficient use of such space in peacetime as well as during wars, as is the case of the below-ground hospital that we researched in Shanghai.

In spite of strict control, there is slow, steady, urbanization in China. With the "four modernizations" (industry, agriculture, science and technology, and defense), I anticipate that such a movement will accelerate. Adding to this urbanization is the rapid improvement in the Chinese standard of living, especially for farmers, and the increased consumption of transportation and urban services. In any case urbanization in China takes place in a more orderly manner than in any other developing country. Urbanization, however, has two correlated dimensions: population growth and increased space consumption. The latter applies to

two major types: dwellings and services (such as entertainment, education, management, offices) and employment (industry and other production). From this very practical approach, Chinese urban designers and planners regard urban below-ground space as a valuable natural resource. Such land use is particularly adaptable in certain cities such as Beijing, Shanghai, Chongqing, and Nanjing.

In this book a distinction is made between villages, which are defined as small agrarian communities, and cities, considered to be large-scale, nonagricultural communities of varying sizes. The words *village* and *city* have been added to the place names to aid in this distinction but are not to be considered part of the official name.

This volume covers almost all aspects and ac-

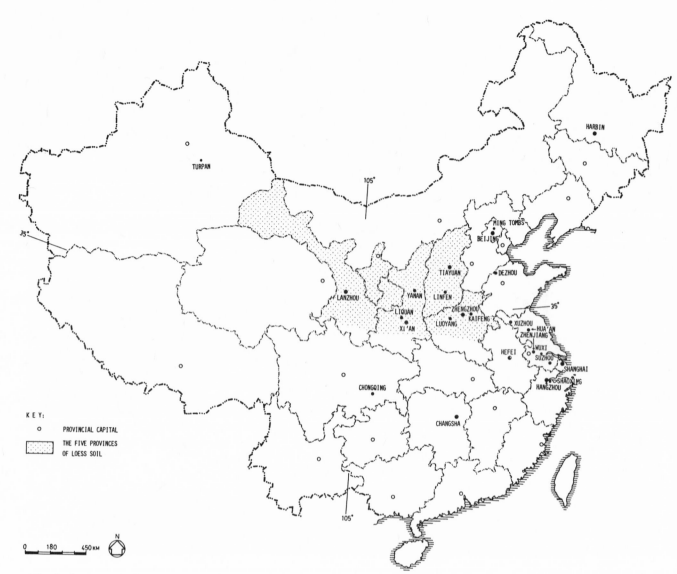

Fig. 3. Important places mentioned in this book where below-ground space has been in use, especially in urban centers.

tivities of below-ground nonresidential space in China. As such it certainly fills a long-overdue gap in the literature in English (fig. 3). Much of the innovative contemporary practice of the diversified below-ground space usage in China is a continuation of the traditional historical de-velopment and uses the same principles and ex-periences. As the old Chinese saying has it, "There is nothing that heaven does not cover and nothing that earth does not sustain" (Chuange Tzu, 369–286 B.C.

1

Ancient and Vernacular Practice

TEMPLES AND TOMBS

One of the most ancient uses of below-ground space in China was for burial. Tombs are scattered all over China in the form of artificial hills that reveal themselves from afar. Some of the tombs have been opened and many others are still covered by earth. Common to almost every one of them is an impressive avenue of huge stone sculptures representing an emperor's officers, animals, or imaginative creatures. Also Buddhist temples were often built within the cliffs, with sculptures of Buddha and his followers carved in stone (fig. 4).

Most of the ancient noble Chinese families were buried more than 10 meters below-ground. The walls of the grave were completely coated by alternate layers of white clay and charcoal. A thick layer of earth on top of the grave helped maintain constant temperature and moisture inside in a perfectly antiseptic environment. In Changsha city of Hunan Province, a woman's body buried two thousand years ago under such conditions was found preserved in excellent condition.[1]

Qianling Tomb on Mount Liangshan, Qian Xian County, Shaanxi Province, is the joint tomb of Emperor Gaozong (628–683) and Empress Wu Zetian (624–705) of the Tang dynasty. There are also seventeen minor tombs in the vicinity,

several of which have been excavated. Visible in these tombs are well-preserved murals, stone sculptures of humans and animals, carved pillars and steles, and glazed pottery.[2]

MING TOMBS

One of the most famous tomb complexes known in China is the Ming tombs. They are located around 10 kilometers from Changping, a new-town satellite north of Beijing. They are distributed within a 40-square kilometer basin and are known as Shisanling or the thirteen Ming tombs (fig. 5). Each of these tombs is an elaborate architecturally designed below-ground space.

The basin itself is surrounded by mountain ridges on the east, north, and west, leaving the south as a gateway. Like similar entrances, the Dagongmen Gate is flanked by Dragon Hill and Tiger Hill, which guard the tomb area (fig. 6). The Wenyu River meanders through from the northwest. The Ming tombs were built over more than two centuries. Construction of the Chang Ling tomb was begun in 1409 for Emperor Cheng Zu. The other twelve were built in succeeding years, ending in 1644 when the Ming dynasty was overthrown.

The sixteen emperors of the Ming dynasty were in power for 277 years (1368–1644). Zhu Di (Cheng Zu) was emperor when Nanjing was

Fig. 4. Front view of rock cave Buddhist temple in Gong County, Henan Province.

the capital in 1403, yet he recognized Beiping (Beijing) as a city of strategic importance. He drafted one million craftsmen and laborers for the construction of Beijing, to become the capital of China. He selected the site in the Ming tombs basin especially for Empress Xu when she died. This site was considered ideal because of the surrounding hills, the thickness of the earth, and the imaginative assertions of the geomancers, who said that the hills resembled dragons, tigers, snakes, and tortoises, or the stars, planets, moon, and sun. In short, the site contained the spirit of everything in the universe. Zhu Di placed troops to defend the tombs as well as the capital. The basin includes his own tomb at the foot of Tianshou Hill and another twelve Ming dynasty emperors.

Chang Ling Tomb. Chang Ling is the earliest constructed tomb of the Ming tombs complex where Zhu Di, who reigned from 1403 to 1424 as Emperor Cheng Zu, and Empress Xu were buried.

Chang Ling tomb is very elaborate in design and materials. The front part is square while the rear is circular. There were thirty-two sandalwood pillars in the hall, four of which were 1.17 meters in diameter each. The woodwork is still intact and sturdy after five hundred years. As Jin Shixu, author of *The Ming Tombs*, wrote,

Built on an axis were such main buildings as Lingmen (Gate to the Tomb), Ling'enmen (Gate of Eminent Favours), Ling'endian (Hall of Eminent Favours), Neihongmen (Inner Red Gate), Shifang (Stone Archway) and Minglou (Ming Tower). Annexes were arranged symmetrically on both sides [fig. 7]. Inside the main gate were five Sacred Kitchens on the east (where meals were prepared for those who paid homage to the spirit of the emperor and sacrificial offerings were made) and five Sacred Storehouses on the west (where foodstuffs were stored). Today, no remains of these kitchens and storehouses can be found.

In order to build the tomb an army of craftsmen

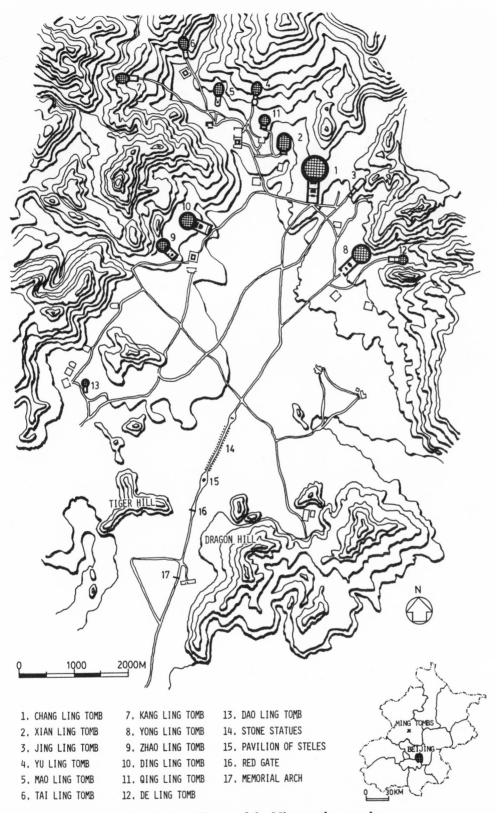

1. CHANG LING TOMB	7. KANG LING TOMB	13. DAO LING TOMB
2. XIAN LING TOMB	8. YONG LING TOMB	14. STONE STATUES
3. JING LING TOMB	9. ZHAO LING TOMB	15. PAVILION OF STELES
4. YU LING TOMB	10. DING LING TOMB	16. RED GATE
5. MAO LING TOMB	11. QING LING TOMB	17. MEMORIAL ARCH
6. TAI LING TOMB	12. DE LING TOMB	

Fig. 5. Overall map of the Ming tombs complex.

Fig. 6. Sculpture avenue leading to ancient tombs near Xi'an city, Shaanxi Province.

and laborers was drafted from nearby provinces to help the soldiers. It took eighteen years to complete the project (1409–27).[3]

Ding Ling Tomb. Ding Ling tomb complex is the most famous, the most visited, and the most extensively excavated complex of the thirteen tombs. It is also the best known emperor's tomb that was built in the late Ming dynasty, construction having started in 1584 and lasting six years. Located at the foot of Xiaoyushan (or Small Valley Hill), later renamed the Dayushan (or Big Valley Hill), it is the tomb of Emperor Shen Zong, who reigned from 1573 to 1620, and his two empresses. His lifestyle was luxurious and extravagant. It was no coincidence that during his time the Ming dynasty became corrupt and declined politically.

The layout of the surface buildings of the Ding Ling tomb is similar to that of Yong Ling tomb and covers an area of 180,000 square meters (fig. 8). Three single-arched bridges of white marble are at the front gate, and at the other end of the bridges is a double-eaved pavilion with steles inside. More than three thousand

cultural relics have been unearthed, including fabrics, jewels, and utensils. Around the pavilion are three hundred bays built for sacrifices and other purposes. The outer gate is fifty steps from the pavilion. The present entrance to the tomb used to be the second gate with five sacred kitchens on the left and five sacred storehouses on the right. Behind the Ming Tower was the Precious Citadel, 270 meters in diameter. The troops of Qing dynasty (1644–1911) destroyed the Ming Ling tomb. However, during the Qian Long period of the Qing dynasty, the Gate of Eminent Favors and the Hall of Eminent Favors were rebuilt to ease national conflicts. In 1914, a fire destroyed most of the surface buildings of the Ding Ling tomb. In 1956 the entrance to the tomb was rediscovered and excavation of the secrets of the palace began.

The underground palace consists of an antechamber, a central chamber with annexes on each side, and a back chamber (fig. 9). The first two chambers are separated by a stone gateway, and a third gateway leads to the back chamber. A pair of stone doors leads to vaulted passages in

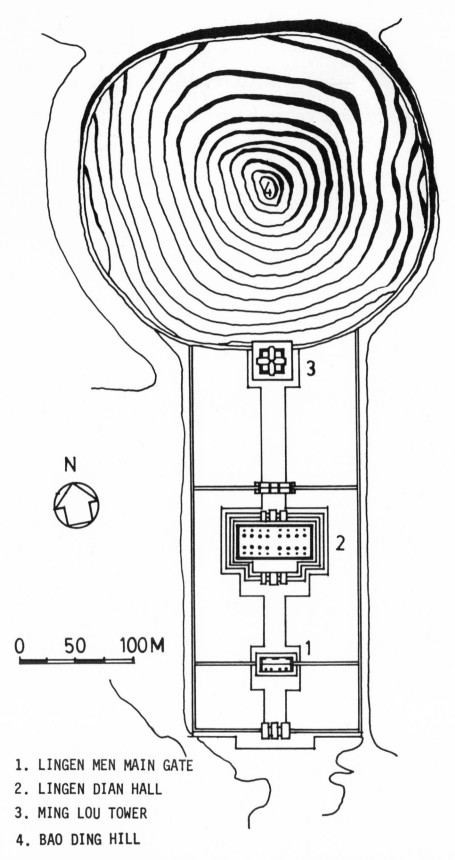

N

0 50 100 M

1. LINGEN MEN MAIN GATE
2. LINGEN DIAN HALL
3. MING LOU TOWER
4. BAO DING HILL

Fig. 7. Plan of the above-ground part of Chang Ling tomb, one of the thirteen Ming tombs. The tomb is still covered with earth.

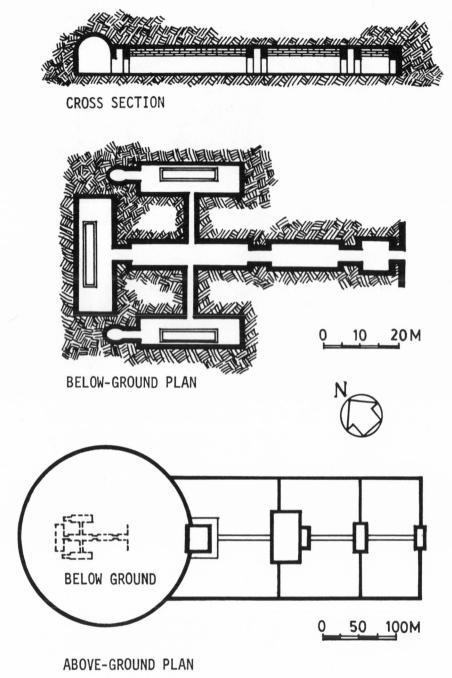

CROSS SECTION

BELOW-GROUND PLAN

0   10   20 M

N

BELOW GROUND

0   50   100M

ABOVE-GROUND PLAN

Fig. 8. Plan of Ding Ling tomb, one of the thirteen Ming tombs.

the west wall of each annex. There are seven gateways and a total of 1,195 square meters of floor space. The underground palace was built entirely of stone with vaulted ceilings and is free of columns or beams. The back chamber, the burial chamber, is the largest and the most important section of the underground palace. Three coffins lie side by side on the stone couch.[4]

GRAIN STORAGE SYSTEMS

A second ancient use of below-ground space in China is that of food storage. This usage is still practical and employed today in China (fig. 10). Underground food storage appeared in China in the Neolithic period. Natural caves dating

Fig. 9. Along the axis of the central chamber of the Ding Ling tomb.

from the Stone Age, such as the one found in Banpo village, located near Xi'an city, were used for below-ground food storage. China has had a long history and much innovative experience in this field. Development of the food storage system in China evolved simultaneously with the rise of agriculture and with the awareness, especially in the semiarid and arid regions, that climatic seasonal changes may cause famine. Thus, the system became a necessity for survival.

BASIC PRINCIPLES

More than any other nation, China derives its contemporary storage from traditional practice combined with modern principles. Except in North America, which uses above-ground round metal or wooden silos for grain storage, the traditional system (and especially the ancient one) has been below ground. Of all the countries of the world, China has the most sophisticated experience in below-ground grain storage.

In 1971, a large ancient grain storage pit was discovered in Luoyang city, Henan Province. Pits of this type were dug in a dry loess soil layer above the water table, then the sides of the pit were beaten and burned with charcoal to make the inner surfaces hard and a coating of waterproof grease was applied. Later the walls were covered with wooden boards and straw mats. After storing the millet between two layers of husks, workers sealed the pit with earth.[5]

In A.D. 605 and 606, near the ancient capital city of Luoyang, several thousand grain pits were constructed in the loess soil by Emperor Yang Kuang of the Sui dynasty. Some of the famous recently excavated Hanjia pits had a total capacity of five hundred thousand tons. A bell-shaped pit evolved that helped insulate against moisture and heat gain and loss; along with the 50 percent lower cost of construction, this type of pit made the below-ground Chinese food storehouse competitive with the comparable above-ground facility. Today below-ground food storage is used outside the loess soil zone all over China. In warm, moist regions below-ground food preservation can be particularly effective. Considerable energy savings are also realized by the use of below-ground refrigeration plants.[6]

Construction of the Hanjia storage pits began

Fig. 10. Below-ground food storage well commonly used by farmers. Cui Mingxing family cave dwelling, Dayang village, east of Linfen city, Shanxi Province.

during the Sui dynasty and continued through the Tang dynasty (A.D. 581–907). The entire storage facility contained 1.25 billion kilograms of grain, which would have fed one million people for seven years. Most of the grain was either millet from northern China or rice from southeast China. This facility was discontinued when Luoyang, the national capital, moved to Xi'an in the tenth century. The Hanjia pits were forgotten until 1971, when records on hundreds of grain pits were discovered. Two hundred and eighty-seven of these pits were located and sixteen of them have been dug out. In one pit researchers found 25 million kilograms of grain, of which 57.2 percent was still recognizable material. This pit (no. 82), 7 meters deep, 13.5 meters in diameter at its top, and 10.5 meters in diameter at the base, is the largest pit yet excavated. In preparing the pit, wood was burned to dry the soil. The floor and the walls were covered with limestone to absorb moisture and tung tree oil was used for waterproofing. The floor was covered with wooden planks (2 to 3 centimeters thick), then rice husks, and finally the pit was filled with rice or millet. Rice husks were

also used to separate one type of grain from another. The grain was covered with layers of straw and matting to absorb moisture, and finally, soil covered the mats. The 287 grain pits differ in size (fig. 11); eleven are now used for scientific research and one is a museum.[7]

In addition to the thermal and environmental benefits of the Chinese traditional system for underground grain storage, other advantages exist as well, such as protection from fire, birds, insects, rodents, and theft by human beings. The Hanjia pits were constructed, maintained, and monitored by the government. Thus their survival was a national priority similar to that of ancient Egypt. It is worth mentioning that modern China uses similar methods of below-ground grain storage for similar reasons: survival, defense, quality, and low construction costs.

TEMPERATURE FOR FOOD STORAGE

The loess soil region of northern and northwestern China has a long tradition of below-ground storage of grain, vegetables, fruit, sweet potatoes, and other agricultural products. Our

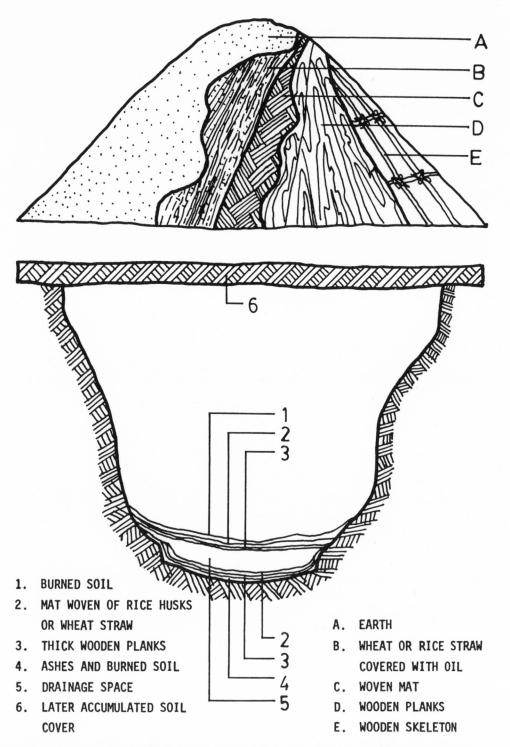

1. BURNED SOIL
2. MAT WOVEN OF RICE HUSKS
   OR WHEAT STRAW
3. THICK WOODEN PLANKS
4. ASHES AND BURNED SOIL
5. DRAINAGE SPACE
6. LATER ACCUMULATED SOIL
   COVER

A. EARTH
B. WHEAT OR RICE STRAW
   COVERED WITH OIL
C. WOVEN MAT
D. WOODEN PLANKS
E. WOODEN SKELETON

Fig. 11. Crosssection sketch of the Hanjia below-ground grain pit no. 58 discovered in Luoyang, the ancient Chinese capital.

research in central Gansu Province in the loess soil zone points out that during midsummer, when outdoor temperatures reached more than 35 degrees C (95 degrees F) in the afternoon and fluctuated to a low of 10 degrees C (50 degrees F) after midnight, the below-ground indoor temperature was diurnally stable, at around 16 degrees C (60 degrees F). In the winter, when the outdoor temperature fell below 0 degrees C (32 degrees F), the average diurnal indoor temperature was stable around 10 degrees C (50 degrees F).

At Yan'an city in north Shaanxi Province, our findings show that during mid-July, when the outdoor relative humidity was around 95 percent, the indoor below-ground humidity was almost stable at around 80 percent. On the other hand, the relative humidity in early January was almost stable at 60 percent. Below-ground facilities have proven to be advantageous for storage of food under such ambient temperatures. The seasonal and diurnal stability of temperature and relative humidity contribute significantly to food preservation.

A comparative experiment in storing rice below ground and above ground for nine months was conducted at Chongqing city, outside the loess zone. There were considerable changes in the above-ground rice. Moisture content was higher and the rice discolored slightly. The underground rice did not change, in fact it retained 22 percent more carbohydrate content than the above-ground sample. Also, pests infested the above-ground rice two to three months earlier than that below ground. In the below-ground granary pest infestation was controlled by vacuuming with an air pump. The study concludes that underground granaries are safe even in the hot summer, free from bacterial growth, do not cause discoloration of the rice or self-heating of the grain, do not require pesticides, and cause grain to decay at a much slower rate than in the above-ground storage. The study also points out that underground granaries are easier to manage and have 25 percent lower maintenance costs than above-ground granaries.[8]

THE PIT GRANARY

Chinese underground pit granary practice has more than four thousand years of accumulated experience. The principles of this method can be summarized as follows:

Stable Environment. Below-ground ambient environment provides almost stable diurnal and seasonal temperatures. Under special circumstances the effect of the outdoor air temperature can become zero diurnally and minimal seasonally. Grain can be preserved when its metabolic process is stopped during storage. Otherwise the increased heat will stimulate activity in the embryos and accelerated deterioration will take place. Thus the temperature and the relative humidity need to be stable.[9] This is exactly the condition which the below-ground environment provides. The ideal temperature is 15 degrees C (59 degrees F) or below. In the tropics, where temperatures exceed 25 to 45 degrees C (77 to 113 degrees F), cooling is necessary.[10] This is why the northern (and to some extent the central) part of China is most suitable for underground pit grain storage.

Air Exchange. Since the system is airtight and compact, it does not allow air exchange and therefore eliminates insects and bacteria. Depletion of oxygen in the container kills those organisms that depend on oxygen, mainly insects and most fungi, before they can damage the grain.[11]

Moisture. Moisture content of the grain is 13 to 14 percent or less during the storage time. Harvested grain usually contains 20 to 30 percent moisture. Thus the grain must be dried before storage. Equilibrium moisture is the balance between the grain moisture content and the water vapor in the surrounding air. The arid and semiarid parts of northern China, where average air humidity is low during most of the year, are suitable for below-ground pit storage.

Water Table. All underground grain storage pits are constructed above the level of the water table in order to minimize humidity.

Waterproofing. To prevent water and humidity penetration, the below-ground pit surface was paved, sometimes with bricks, then covered with limestone and a powerful drying oil (obtained from the tung tree), followed by wooden planks and rice husk matting. After the pit was filled with grain, workers placed layers on top that consisted of a wooden skeleton (or framework), wooden planks, rice husk mats, then straw (about 10 centimeters thick), more tung oil, and finally, earth (fig. 8).[12]

Outlet. In the case of modern pits, a tunnel is constructed at the lowest point to allow for removal and transportation of grain.

Monitoring Bacteria. Monitoring the bacteria and insect activity of the storage environment is necessary during the storage period. Today the Chinese, using microseismic techniques, listen to the stored grain for any indication of deterioration. If found, they inject very small quantities of fumigant to kill the bacteria and prevent decay.[13]

Advantages. The traditional Chinese granary system is the underground pit type. Similar methods were used in many other regions of the world, including the Middle East, North Africa, all over Asia, and in semidry and dry climatic zones. The significant advantages of the underground pit method are:

1. Long-term storage that can retain grain quality for decades or even hundreds of years, if treated properly.
2. Reduces the process of grain decay.
3. Low maintenance costs.
4. Relatively simple construction using low technology and, compared with the aboveground silo, does not require sophisticated engineering.
5. Requires a minimum of building materials. Uses materials that are commonly found in China, except for the wood.
6. Eliminates or minimizes insects, bacteria, fungi, rats, and rodents.
7. Keeps grain safe under insecure conditions (war or vandalism).

In spite of all its advantages, the traditional pit method is difficult to handle (especially to empty). Inventory is hard to control and the pits are difficult to reach. Nevertheless most of these limitations can be overcome by improved design.

HENAN GRANARIES

More than five thousand years ago the Chinese used underground caverns that were wide at the bottom and narrow at the top for food storage. Until A.D. 907 they stored food in this way on a large scale. In A.D. 605, Emperor Sui Yang built the Hanjia town storehouse at Luoyang city. In 606, with the relocation of the capital, a new below-ground storage called Xingluo was built at Luokou (also called Luokou

storehouse) which is located on the plateau in southeast Gong County, Henan Province. The city was surrounded by walls and had three thousand large below-ground granaries, each one capable of storing more than 500 million kilograms of grain.

Another below-ground grain storage area, located 3.5 kilometers north of Luoyang city, is called Huilou. There are around three hundred large-scale granaries in this region. Both the Luokou and Hanjia granaries were discovered in Luoyang city in 1971.[14]

LUOYANG CITY GRANARIES

Luoyang city in the northwestern part of Henan Province, the East Capital of China, was constructed by the emperors of the Sui and Tang dynasties (A.D. 581–907). The name East Capital was given to the city in order to distinguish it from the West Capital, Changan (Xi'an today). During the Sui and Tang dynasties, Luoyang was very prosperous and played an important role in the history of China. The city is located near the banks of the Yellow River, surrounded by mountains, fertile loess soil, plenty of water, and has a moderate climate with warm rainy summers and cold, almost dry winters. The surroundings constitute part of the region known as the cradle of Chinese civilization. Nine ancient dynasties selected Luoyang as their capital; accordingly it was called "Capital of Nine Dynasties."[15]

The East Capital was constructed by Emperor Suiyang to enhance his dominant position as emperor while the food storage center was planned to supply the army. The Luoyang site itself has a favorable geopolitical position. The West Capital (Xi'an) was an agricultural center but could not meet the needs of the population, so famine caused the government to move alternately between Luoyang and Xi'an. In addition, Luoyang has river transportation and a somewhat higher summer precipitation than the West Capital. The construction of the East Capital, which began in January 605, involved more than two million workers. By March 606 it was finished and in April Emperor Suiyang entered the city with his nobles and officials.

Luoyang, the East Capital, consisted of a large number of blocks (fig. 12). At the northwestern corner is the Emperor's Forbidden City (Gong City) complex, which is composed of seven towns (fig. 13): Emperor's Palace, Emperor's Town,

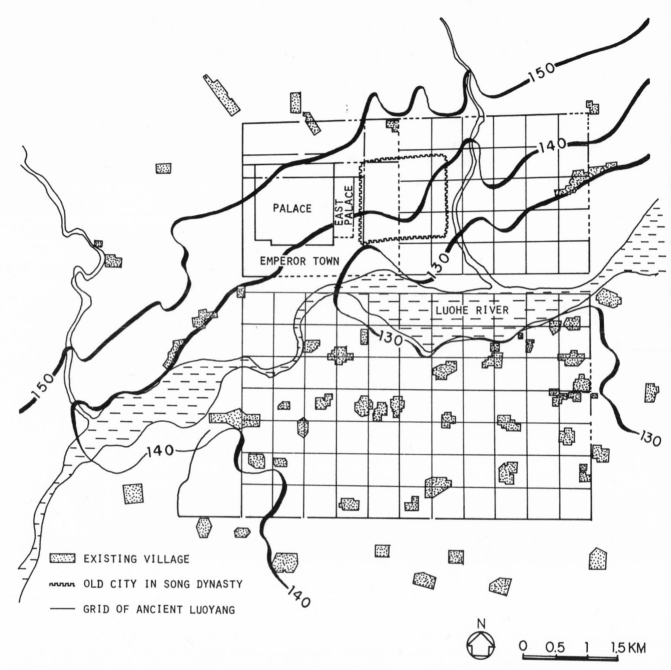

Fig. 12. General plan of Luoyang (East Capital), and the northwestern complex of the Emperor's Palaces and towns, the Hanjia town, and the ancient city wall of the Song dynasty.

East Palace, East town, Hanjia town, Yuanbi town, and Quyi town. The city has a rammed earth wall 15 to 16 meters thick. There are two to four gates in each direction. In 606 there were 202,000 families in East Capital Luoyang; assuming that the average family consists of five persons, the total population probably numbered more than one million (Fuwei and Guanbao, 3–8).

HANJIA TOWN

Hanjia town was built as one of the seven subdivisions of East Capital Luoyang. Hanjia town is connected with the Mang Mountains to the north and with the north wall of the old city on the south. The Longhai railway now passes through the area in an east-west direction. The

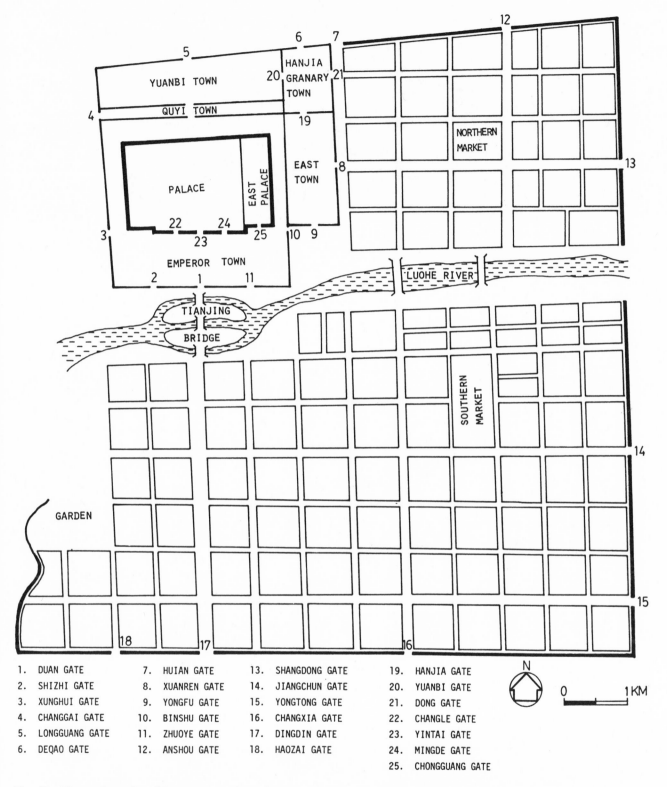

1.	DUAN GATE	7.	HUIAN GATE	13.	SHANGDONG GATE	19.	HANJIA GATE
2.	SHIZHI GATE	8.	XUANREN GATE	14.	JIANGCHUN GATE	20.	YUANBI GATE
3.	XUNGHUI GATE	9.	YONGFU GATE	15.	YONGTONG GATE	21.	DONG GATE
4.	CHANGGAI GATE	10.	BINSHU GATE	16.	CHANGXIA GATE	22.	CHANGLE GATE
5.	LONGGUANG GATE	11.	ZHUOYE GATE	17.	DINGDIN GATE	23.	YINTAI GATE
6.	DEQAO GATE	12.	ANSHOU GATE	18.	HAOZAI GATE	24.	MINGDE GATE
						25.	CHONGGUANG GATE

Fig. 13. The ancient city of Luoyang consists of a large number of huge blocks distributed south and north of the Luohe River. At the northwestern corner is the Emperor's Forbidden City. This complex is made of the Emperor's Palaces, Emperor's Town, East town, Hanjia town, Yuanbi town, and Quyi town.

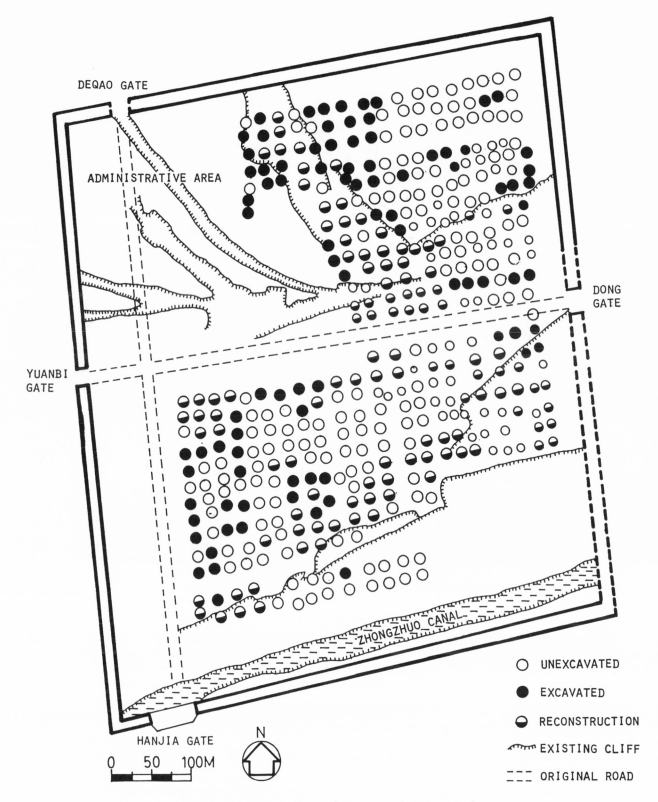

DEQAO GATE

ADMINISTRATIVE AREA

YUANBI
GATE

DONG
GATE

HANJIA GATE

N

ZHONGZHUO CANAL

0   50   100M

○ UNEXCAVATED

● EXCAVATED

◐ RECONSTRUCTION

⌒⌒⌒ EXISTING CLIFF

— — — ORIGINAL ROAD

Fig. 14. Hanjia granary town. There are 412 storage pits.

Hanjia granary, located within the East Capital, has made Luoyang city the most experienced in food storage in China. Moreover, much of the contemporary and modern Chinese experience in below-ground food storage is based on the ancient practices of Henan Province, especially those of the Luoyang city region (Fuwei and Guanbao, 1).

In the eastern and southern parts of Hanjia town some four hundred oval or circular underground pit granaries of different sizes have been discovered (fig. 14). Today some of them are below the railway or other buildings. As figure 14 shows, there are no such granaries in the northwestern part of the city, which may have been used for administration. Also discovered were two wide roads going north-south and east-west.

Hanjia town walls are on the east, north, and west sides. The southern side of the town is attached to the northern walls of ancient Luoyang city (of the period of the Sui dynasty), which form a trapezoid. The north wall is 612 meters long, 17 meters wide, and the height varies from 1.5 to 3 meters. The east wall starts from the northeastern corner of the town and continues south to merge with the ancient wall of Luoyang city. The western wall, which is shared with Yuanbi town and is largely covered by modern structures, is 710 meters long, 15 meters wide, and 1 to 2.5 meters high (fig. 13). The total area covered by Hanjia town is approximately 430,000 square meters.

Hanjia town has four gates: Hanjia gate to the south, Deqao gate to the north, Yuanbi gate to the west, and the Dong or Eastern gate in the eastern wall. This last gate may have been the entrance to the town from the river. Hanjia gate is not yet excavated, but Deqao wall has been partly uncovered. The Deqao gate is 17 meters long, the same as the width of the city wall (Fuwei and Guanbao, 10–16).

Hanjia Granaries. In 749 the Hanjia granaries stored about 12 million kilograms of grain. The second largest granary center of the Tang dynasty, it managed primarily husked and unhusked rice. The sources of the grain were Shuzhou, Chuzhou, and Tuzhou in southern China, and Jizhou, Xinzhou, Dezhou, Fuzhou, Changzhou, and Weizhou in the north (Fuwei and Guanbao, 3).

The Qinling Mountains divide northern and southern China. Thus Luoyang and the Hanjia granaries occupied a strategic position at the center of the area, which lay between the colder, arid, and semiarid millet-growing north and the warmer, more humid, rice-growing south. The two parts of the country, although climatically different, complement each other economically. A ruler would covet both the East and West capitals in order to defend himself against enemy invasions.

The Hanjia granaries are a complex of pits organized in east-west, north-south rows. The pits look like circular jars, large at the top and narrow at the bottom (fig. 14). The largest opening is 18 meters wide and it is 12 meters deep. The smallest is 8 meters by 6 meters (Fuwei and Guanbao, 4). The distribution pattern of the below-ground pit granaries is very dense. Until the early 1980s 287 pit granaries had been discovered but experts estimate that there are more than four hundred, all located in the northeastern and the southern parts of Hanjia town. The average distance between arrays is 6 to 8 meters (some are 3 meters and a few are 15 meters apart). The distance between pits is 3 to 5 meters with a few less than 2 meters (Fuwei and Guanbao, 20).

Although the diameter of the largest pit is 18 meters, the usual opening is 10 to 16 meters, with a depth of usually 7 to 9 meters. Some pits have a diameter of 2.7 meters and a depth of 4.5 meters, which suggests that the Hanjia granaries were built at different times (fig. 15). The excavators conclude that the shapes, structures, and construction procedures were basically similar to each other. Some pits were discovered full of grain. The average storage capacity of one pit granary is 5 to 6 million Chinese jing, or about 2.5 million kilograms (Fuwei and Guanbao, 57).

Construction begins at the top with an oval or circular opening. The walls curve outward in the midsection and lead to a narrow curved or flat bottom. Then the walls and the bottom are smoothed. Every pit has a small curved ditch at the bottom, 1 meter long, .5 meters wide, and .3 meters deep at the deepest point, the purpose of which is still not known. Waterproofing measures were taken during the excavation (fig. 15). On the bottom and the side walls, waterproofing was reinforced by covering them with a layer of dry soil (2 to 4 centimeters thick), ramming the soil, drying by burning wood and leaving the ash to reduce moisture, coating with a layer of a drying agent of oil taken from the tung tree (a traditional material broadly used in ancient China against moisture), and covering with in-

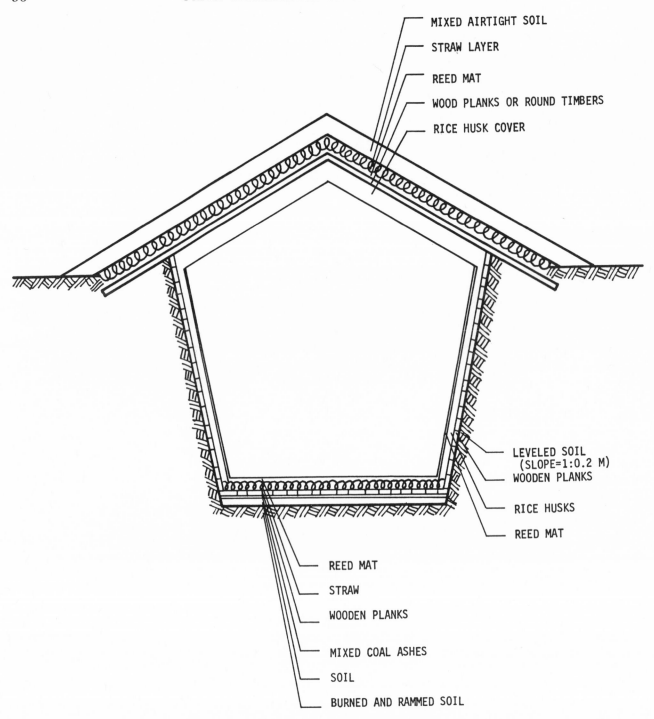

Fig. 15. Crosssection of grain pit in Hanjia town.

terlocking or parallel wooden planks, straw, husks, reeds, or other interwoven matting material (Fuwei and Guanbao, 20–24).

A roof covers the pit when it is filled completely. This roof is made of mats and 40 to 60 centimeters of rice husks in alternate layers and then sealed by loess soil heaped up in a cone shape. Similar sealing methods were used in rural China until 1949, especially in Henan Province. Another method is sealing with alternate layers of mats and straw, bamboo pieces, wood bars, wood plants, and so on. The mat is fixed on a wooden frame with bamboo strings, and a layer of straw 10 centimeters thick covers the mat. The straw and soil layer were painted for waterproofing. In a pit 10 meters in diameter a timber column is added at the center to support the umbrella-shaped roof. This type of roof, however, was discovered outside the Hanjia town storage while the exact roofing method of the town pit granary has not yet been discovered. The entrance to the pit was probably higher than the ground surface and the pit roof was made larger for effective drainage (Fuwei and Guanbao, 26–29).

Management of Hanjia Granaries. Information on the method of management of the Hanjia granaries is known through the carved bricks found in the pit granaries. Each pit has recorded the quantity of grain, time of storage, and names of the officials involved. The transportation process was also marked on the bricks (Fuwei and Guanbao, 29–33). The granaries were a government enterprise and of national concern. The Hanjia granary does not have any historical record that would indicate its importance before the Sui dynasty, nor during this dynasty did it become a major governmentally managed food storage center. All the carved bricks recording the usage and the development of Hanjia town granary are from the Tang dynasty (Fuwei and Guanbao, 48).

Rice, millet, and some red beans were the major products stored during the Sui and Tang dynasties. In addition to the East Capital's Hanjia granaries, there were other major granaries as well during this time such as the West Capital Xi'an's Taichang granaries, Huazhou's Yongfeng and Guangtong granaries, and Shaanzhou's Taiyuan granaries (fig. 16) (Fuwei and Guanbao, 35, 44). At the Hanjia town granaries the pits number 160 and 2.5 million kilograms of millet still remain.

Transportation of grain was primarily by canal. During the Sui dynasty millions of people were brought in to excavate the Great Canal, which extended north-south in the eastern part of China. The purpose of this canal was to strengthen the control of the dynasty in eastern China and East Capital Luoyang and consequently to explore further the resources of this immense region.

The grain income brought to Hanjia town was primarily based on the land taxation system of the government. This was also a traditional Chinese ruler's way to exploit the farmers. Both the Sui and Tang dynasties used the Equal Land System. This system divided the land among adult males according to their status. Males at the age of eighteen to twenty were called middle male, those aged twenty-one to fifty-nine were called Ding male (subject to military service), and men aged sixty and more were called old male. Each middle and Ding male could receive 3.29 acres under this system plus an additional 13.18 acres of government land on the condition that a percentage of its production had to be given to the emperor. Old and invalid males received 6.59 acres each and widows and secondary wives received 4.94 acres per person, again with a percentage of produce going to the government. The land was divided among nobles, governmental officials, and farmers. The latter usually received the worst land. According to the Equal Land System each male had to pay a yearly land tax of millet and provide some labor. Land tax applied to the farmers but not to the officials or the nobles. Land of the nobles and officials was also rented to the farmers, as a result the farmers took the full brunt of the land tax (Fuwei and Guanbao, 37–40).

The main system used for transportation was water (rivers and canals) to the capital (Luoyang), where the Hanjia granaries were located. The construction of the Great Canal was combined with the building of the East Capital during the Sui dynasty. Ten million people were called from Henan and Hubei provinces to construct the Great Canal (fig. 17). The Great Canal begins at Luoyang city, connects Luo He and Gu He with the Yellow River, then follows the old Lingdang Canal, which was constructed one thousand years earlier in 770–476 B.C., and flows past Kaifeng to Chuzhou. In A.D. 610 Emperor Suiyang extended the canal south of the Yangtse River to the Qiantang River. The southern extension (Tongji Canal) is about 400 kilometers long and 30 meters wide. With this water network grain and other materials were transported from southeastern China to the East Capital. This canal played a decisive role in economic and cultural exchange.

In 608 the Yongji Canal, which leads north-south, was constructed. More than 1,000 kilometers long, it reaches the Yu River in the south and flows parallel to the Yellow River in the north. This canal connected Yuhang in the south with Luoyang. Because of its importance it

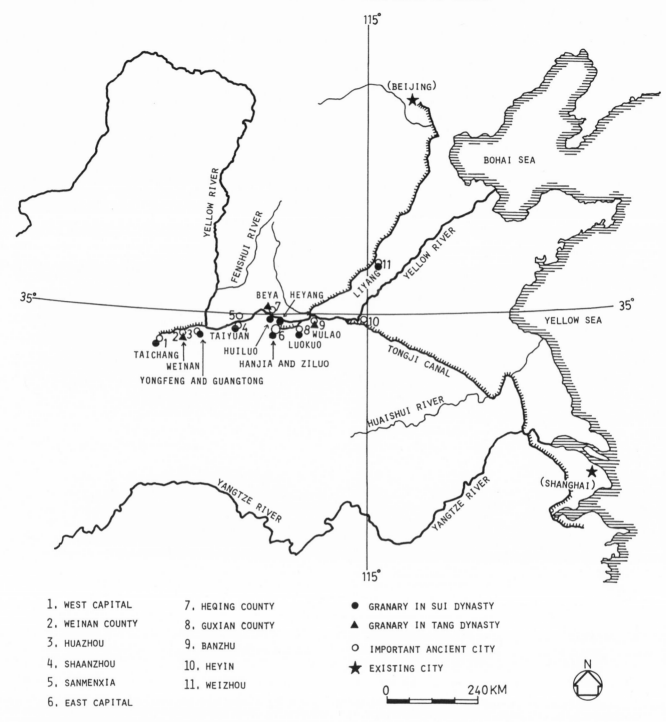

1. WEST CAPITAL
2. WEINAN COUNTY
3. HUAZHOU
4. SHAANZHOU
5. SANMENXIA
6. EAST CAPITAL
7. HEQING COUNTY
8. GUXIAN COUNTY
9. BANZHU
10. HEYIN
11. WEIZHOU

● GRANARY IN SUI DYNASTY
▲ GRANARY IN TANG DYNASTY
○ IMPORTANT ANCIENT CITY
★ EXISTING CITY

0   240 KM

N

Fig. 16. Hanjia town granaries and other regional below-ground granaries in central and eastern China at the time of the Sui and Tang dynasties.

is called the north canal (Fuwei and Guanbao, 41–43). The Tang dynasty strengthened the water transportation network, bringing many socioeconomic changes.

With the construction of the Great Canal Luoyang became a center for north-south water transportation and a temporary grain storage area before the grain moved to Changan (Xi'an) city. However, since the Great Canal consisted of different water courses carrying different quan-

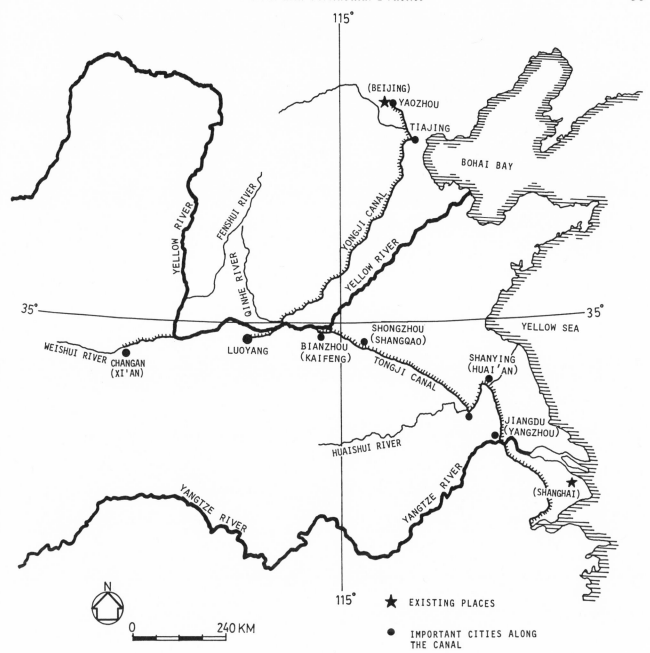

Fig. 17. Water transportation network of the Sui and Tang dynasties and the major stations used for grain transportation.

tities of water at various seasons, water transportation was often disrupted. Consequently there was a need to build temporary granary centers along the water system that would be used before the grain reached its final destination (fig. 18).

Before the Sui dynasty, granary centers had been developed along the Yellow River. They were the Heyang granary in Lanzhou, the Changpin granary in Shaanzhou, the Guangtong granary in Huanzhou, and the Liyang granary in Weizhou. The Tang dynasty rulers also constructed several additional granaries along the water transportation network such as Wulao, which was located at the confluence of the Bi and Yellow rivers, the Beya granary at Heqing, and the Weinan granary in Weinan County (Fuwei and Guanbao, 44, 49). In the ten-year rule of Emperor Wu of the Tang dynasty, Luoyang became the real capital and the Hanjia town granaries became a national food storage center.

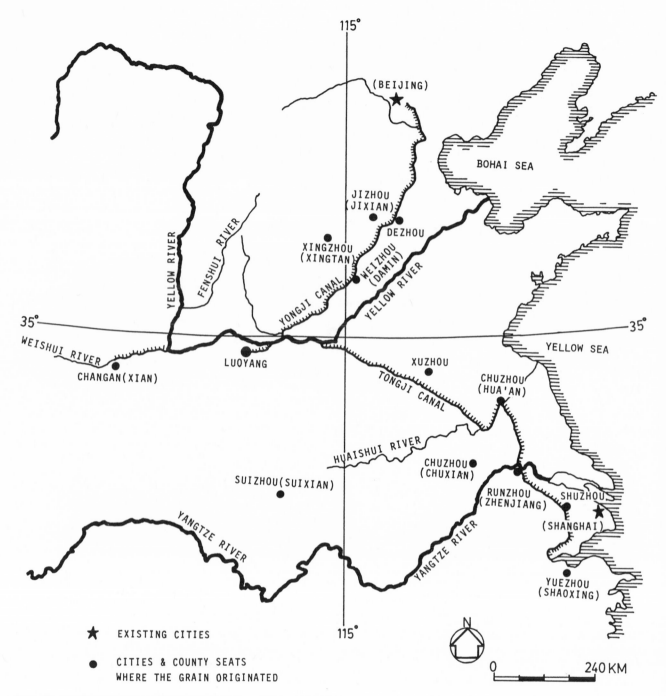

115°

(BEIJING) ★

BOHAI SEA

JIZHOU
(JIXIAN)

DEZHOU

XINGZHOU
(XINGTAN)

WEIZHOU
(DAMIN)

YELLOW RIVER

YONGJI CANAL

YELLOW RIVER

FENSHUI RIVER

35°   35°

WEISHUI RIVER

YELLOW SEA

CHANGAN(XIAN)

LUOYANG

XUZHOU

TONGJI CANAL

CHUZHOU
(HUA'AN)

HUAISHUI RIVER

SUIZHOU(SUIXIAN)

CHUZHOU
(CHUXIAN)

RUNZHOU
(ZHENJIANG)

SHUZHOU

YANGTZE RIVER

(SHANGHAI) ★

YANGTZE RIVER

YUEZHOU
(SHAOXING)

★   EXISTING CITIES

●   CITIES & COUNTY SEATS
    WHERE THE GRAIN ORIGINATED

115°

N

0   240 KM

Fig. 18. Settlements in regions where rice originated and later was stored in Hanjia granaries (Luoyang). Note the water network and the Great Canal for transportation.

2
Contemporary Design

BELOW-GROUND FOOD STORAGE

Before 1949 common houses and temples used below-ground food storage. Most of them did not meet the high standards necessary for successful storage because of the small space available and bad conditions present. The 1965 meeting held by the Chinese Grain Ministry in Shanmenxia, Henan Province, has become a landmark for the construction of modern below-ground space for food preservation. This meeting was followed by the construction of seven types of underground food storage facilities for research and experimentation. In March 1972 another national meeting was held by the Chinese Commercial Ministry at Luoyang city entitled the "Underground Circular Barn" at which the construction of the seven underground storehouses in Henan Province was examined. The loudspeaker-shaped storage facility was widely praised and named Underground Circular Barn. Its counterpart has been constructed in many provinces.[1] Both meetings helped to create a national awareness of the significance of below-ground food storage and of China's wealth of ancient and vernacular practice in this field. The 1950s through the 1970s can be viewed as a period of revival of old experience while using modern design.

Much of modern practice has focused on the development of granaries for pragmatic reasons,

since Chinese nutrition generally comes from rice, millet, wheat, beans, and other grains. There has been impressive achievement in modern methods of storing fruits and vegetables, such as in Chongqing city of Sichuan Province.

Chinese practice has demonstrated that the circular shape (the so-called loudspeaker shape) is the best form for a granary because of its simplicity of construction, low cost, and safety features.[2] Henan Province accumulated a wealth of experience in the development of below-ground grain storage during the 1960s and 1970s. Ten years later those facilities proved to be successful when the stored grain was found to be in good condition. Henan also recorded similar experiences in ancient times as well.

The accelerated movement toward the use of below-ground space for food storage, especially grain storage, in the 1960s was strongly motivated by the tension between the USSR and China at that time. Due to their historical experience this method seemed safer to the Chinese in the event of war.

Today there are three basic types of granary design in China. (fig. 19):

1. Completely underground
2. Semi-below-ground
3. Earth-sheltered, above ground.[3]

Yet old methods of grain treatment are still used in rural China. For example, threshing

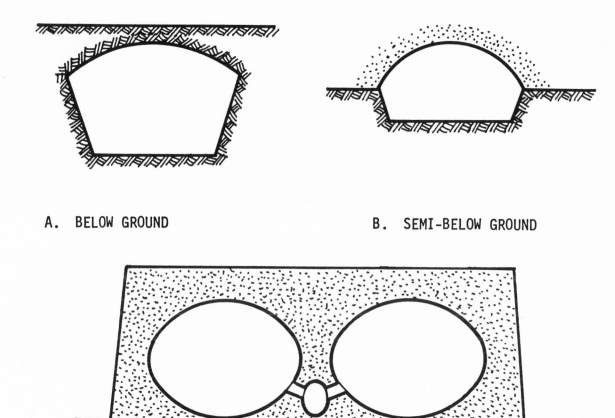

A. BELOW GROUND   B. SEMI-BELOW GROUND

C. EARTH SHELTERED

Fig. 19. Three different forms of earth-integrated granary: below-ground, semi-below-ground and earth-sheltered above-ground.

grain and dehydrating is accomplished on the asphalt surface of roads and takes a few days of intensive labor. The threshing process is performed by wheeled vehicles passing over the stalks (fig. 20).

MODERN GRANARY CONCEPTS

At the underground storage space and granary in the city of Taiyuan, the capital of Shanxi Province, where wheat was stored for ten years, there was no sprouting, insects or worms, mold or deterioration. In other cases vegetables, fruit, and other foods stored in special underground wells remained fresh without decay much longer than those stored above ground. Also chickens raised in caves on the average live a year longer than chickens raised above ground. Hens also

produce twenty to thirty more eggs each per year. In Hongtang County, Shanxi, researchers claim that hens raised in holes dug under heated brick beds in a cave dwelling produce larger eggs continuously year round. Some Chinese practice also points out that cave-raised chickens are more resistant to diseases.[4]

Modern Chinese underground granary construction is based on traditional methods and has proved to be less expensive than above-ground granaries. Two shapes are commonly used: the oval and the spherical, with the former the preferred type. The modern granary near Kaifeng city, Henan, is made of brick with an opening at the top for an entrance and a tunnel at the bottom as an exit. The granary is sealed with bitumen-type materials for waterproofing and to make it airtight.[5] Each bin is 10 meters wide and

Fig. 20. Grain drying on the surface of the road. This method is still commonly used, especially in central and northern China.

14 meters deep and can store approximately 500 metric tons of wheat. The granary is sealed at the entry to keep the relative humidity at 70 to 75 percent. Sound amplification monitors insect activity, and insects are eliminated by gas. The granary is built by the cut-and-cover method and as such is the first of its kind in China. By 1982 this granary had held wheat for four years.[6]

BASIC PRINCIPLES

The modern Chinese below-ground granary has certain significant advantages. They are:

1. Temperature: the winter temperature is usually 10 degrees C (50 degrees F) when the granary is closed tightly. In any case the temperature does not exceed 20 degrees C (68 degrees F) during the year, which is cold enough for grain survival. The range of temperature in the middle and the bottom layers of grain is only 4 to 6 degrees C (39 to 43 degrees F). In the upper layer the fluctuation is higher.

2. Moisture: moisture and relative humidity are kept at lower than 60 to 70 percent. There are a few sources of moisture that may appear in the granary. One is the grain itself, which contains some moisture, and the others are external moisture seeping into the granary or relative humidity penetrating through the ventilation system.

3. Air: an airtight structure with an absence of oxygen keeps the grain in good condition. The reproduction of insects is stopped and germs can be controlled effectively. In examining grain stored below ground for ten years researchers found that its sprouting proportion was 97.8 percent, fat was 2.33 percent, protein was 2.64 percent and acid-

ity was 3.68 percent. There were no significant changes in this grain's condition of ten years earlier.[7]

Problems all granaries face are maintaining low moisture content and low temperatures throughout the year. These two difficulties can be resolved technologically in the above-ground granary but at a cost of increased maintenance. Yet the earth can provide favorable conditions at low cost if damp-resistant measures are taken. Freshness of the grain is greater in below-ground storage than in that above ground. In long-range terms the cost of a below-ground granary is lower than that of an above-ground one.[8]

In China various types of underground granaries have been constructed successfully. During the storage process the metabolism of the grain, commonly described as the breathing process, continues. If there is sufficient oxygen the nutritive elements form water and carbon dioxide,

generating heat, which can reduce the grain quality and induce germination, rot, or insect damage because of the increased temperature and moisture. When carbon dioxide and heat are produced, grain loses its freshness. However, if most oxygen in the granary is eliminated the breathing of the grain can continue through the oxygen existing in its molecules. In order to retain grain quality over a prolonged storage period it is necessary to create conditions and take measures that reduce the breathing process but do not eliminate it entirely. The breathing action may be strengthened if the water content exceeds certain limitations. Grain, however, has a great capacity to absorb moisture from the air, so the air relative humidity must be controlled. Wheat, with a moisture content of 14 to 15 percent, indicates weak breathing at 15 degrees C (59 degrees F). Yet it increases sixteen times at 25 degrees C (77 degrees F). If humidity is below 12 percent no breathing takes place, even if the

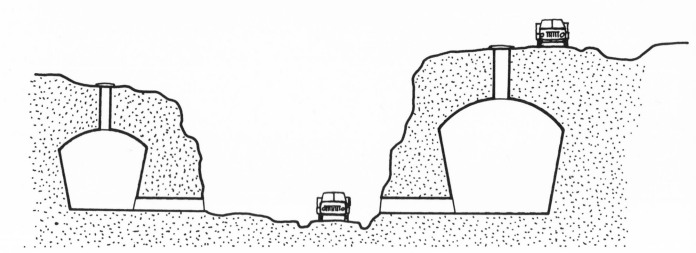

Fig. 21. Location of below-ground granary in loess soil zone.

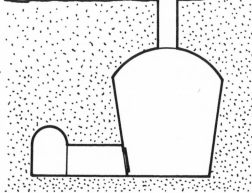

temperature rises to 30 degrees C (86 degrees F). In addition, air movement affects grain breathing as well. Since with an increase in ventilation the breathing also increases, grain temperature must be below 15 degrees C (59 degrees F) or lower, and the relative humidity must be below 75 percent. This requires sealing the storehouse hermetically. Low temperature and relative humidity and the absence of oxygen are essential to prevent the development of insects. Insect damage can be very destructive when temperature and relative humidity are higher than 25 degrees C (77 degrees F) and 85

percent, respectively. The common destructive insects are unable to move in 8 to 15 degrees C (46.5 to 59 degrees F) and they freeze and die in 4 to 8 degrees C (39 to 46.5 degrees F). Rats, sparrows, and the like should be prevented from penetrating into the grain.[9]

The Chinese have designed a comprehensive food storage facility of which the granary is only one part. A granary that is designed to feed ten thousand people for three to four months stores 600,000 kilograms. Some of these granaries are designed as a set of rooms that totals around 500 square meters in floor area; there the grain may

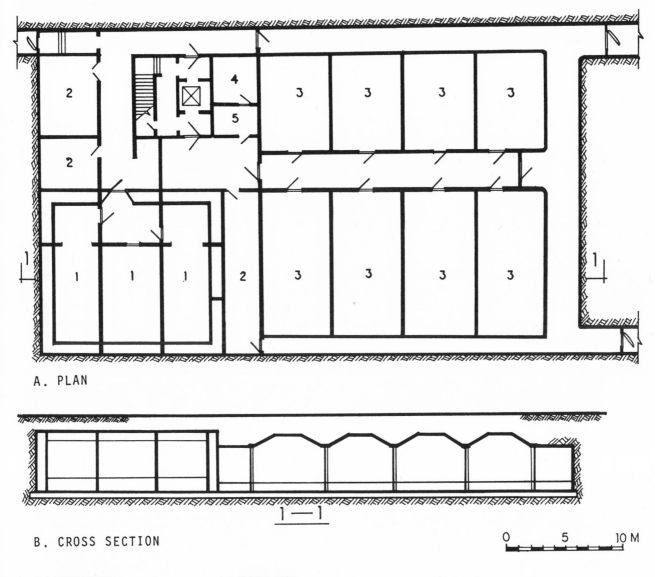

A. PLAN

B. CROSS SECTION

0   5   10 M

1. REFRIGERATOR
2. NON-STAPLE FOOD STOREHOUSE
3. GRANARY
4. BLOWER ROOM
5. OFFICE

Fig. 22. Design of modern below-ground granary complex.

be divided or kept in bulk (fig. 21). The advantage of the latter type is the large storage volume available. The U-shaped granary is found in the loess soil zone and is the traditional Chinese type of storage. It is circular in form but U-shaped in cross-section.

Design principles for below-ground storage should consider the prevention of dampness. The walls and cover should be designed to resist moisture. In modern facilities the inner walls can be isolated from the outer ones by a passageway (fig. 22).

GRANARY SITE SELECTION

Although many of the Chinese granaries have been developed within the loess soil zone because of the significance of the soil quality, there are also many that have been and are being constructed outside this zone. The Chinese policy in granary site allocation has been dispersion rather than concentration for safety and logistical reasons. The Chinese are also very much aware of the contamination threat of above-ground granaries in wartime and the fact that the below-ground facilities can play a significant role in guarding food stuffs at such a time. Moreover, they are very much aware from the historical practice of the economic, social, and qualitative advantages of the below-ground granary.

The basic Chinese approach in site selection for a granary is not to use land suitable for agriculture. They usually select a site on a hill or terraced area, above the water table. The depth of the granary is usually 15 meters, which is six times the height of a common above-ground storehouse.[10] Many underground pit granaries are placed where drainage is favorable. Hanjia town granaries were built near the Mang Mountain, which is high on the north side and low on the south and enabled the site to be well drained and dry.

The Chinese see this stage of site selection as a crucial one. Their criteria are quite comprehensive and varied and include rational layout, favorable landform, suitable soil, low water table, and convenience of water and power sources.[11] A rational layout requires accessibility to transportation, a plan for future growth and expansion, a large area convenient to workers, ability to meet long-range needs, and suitable capacity.

Favorable landforms can apply to alluvial soil, terraces, hilly regions, or plains areas. A terrace is a desirable site because of its good drainage and low water table, especially if it has uniform soil. Hilly land with different landforms can provide good drainage.

In China, soil quality, especially the loess type, has played a major role in the development and usage of below-ground storage spaces in general and the granary in particular. Loess soil is hard when it is dry, almost uniform and without stones, easy to cut, holds its shape well (especially Q1, Q2, and Q3 types), has a low water table, requires only simple tools for digging, and, is generally good for agricultural production. Moreover, loess soil has supported the rise of large-scale construction of below-ground dwellings. The combination of land suitable for agriculture, dwellings, and food storage has helped to bring about the rise of Chinese civilization within the loess soil zone.

A site selected on a slope is more useful than that on a flat area. The Chinese have always used slope sites in order to save flat land for agriculture, for defense, and so on. In any case, using subterranean space does not conflict with other land uses and is basically beneficial. The selection of the slope site will diminish claustrophobia and a lack of direct eye contact with the outdoors. In addition, such subterranean space can use special geological features to greatly reduce the cost of construction. These features can include slopes with alternating horizontal layers of hard and soft rocks (2½ to 5 meters thick) where the soft layer is extracted to create a living space and front terrace. As mentioned earlier, the slopes provide good drainage and ventilation and an attractive surrounding environment. Last, below-ground space on the slopes inflicts the least amount of harm to the natural environment.

GRANARY DESIGN

There are many design types of modern below-ground granaries (figs. 23–28). Most of these forms are an elaboration of the vernacular and ancient designs that are found primarily in the loess soil regions, especially in Henan Province and within the Luoyang city region. Many modern forms were designed and constructed during the 1960s and the 1970s. Since then more experience has been gained from their implementation. This variety of design suits different typographical, drainage, and other special site features (fig. 24).[12]

The most common and most basic design is

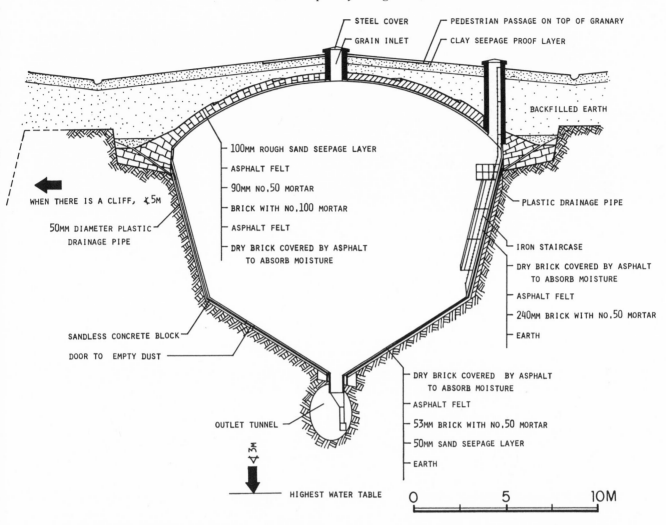

Fig. 23. **Crosssection of the basic design of a modern Chinese below-ground granary. Maximum diameter is 18 meters and maximum depth is 16 meters.**

the reverse bell form (fig. 23). This pit design is similar to the ancient one developed in the Hanjia town granary. This is a large-scale pit with a capacity of 1,500 tons. Other designs on a smaller scale and of simpler form are a semicircle with one common outlet (fig. 25a), a linear form with a single outlet for each pit (fig. 25c), or single pits interconnected and designed in a grid pattern (fig. 25b). In most cases the outlet is designed with a graded tunnel and has an access lower than the actual pit itself. Other types of design are the oval form, which resists side earth pressure (fig. 26), and the parabolic arch (fig. 27). Various arch forms are considered to resist earth pressure (fig. 28). The modern semi-below-ground pit granary form is also utilized in China. Linear small-pit granaries with one outlet have become common for smaller localities (fig.

29). All in all, the last three decades of Chinese activity in below-ground pit granary design have been very fruitful.

LIQUAN COUNTY FOOD STORAGE

In Shaanxi Province, where we conducted research on cave dwellings, we found another type of below-ground food storage facility recently built by Liquan County (fig. 30). All eight storage spaces have been built into a cliff and face a terraced patio; all entrances to the food-storage areas are at this patio level and have large doors facing south toward the sun and the valley. Each space is a long vault that forms a tunnel (fig. 31). At the end of the tunnel is a large vertical chimney for ventilation and air exhange (fig. 32). The inner chimney opening is close to the ceiling

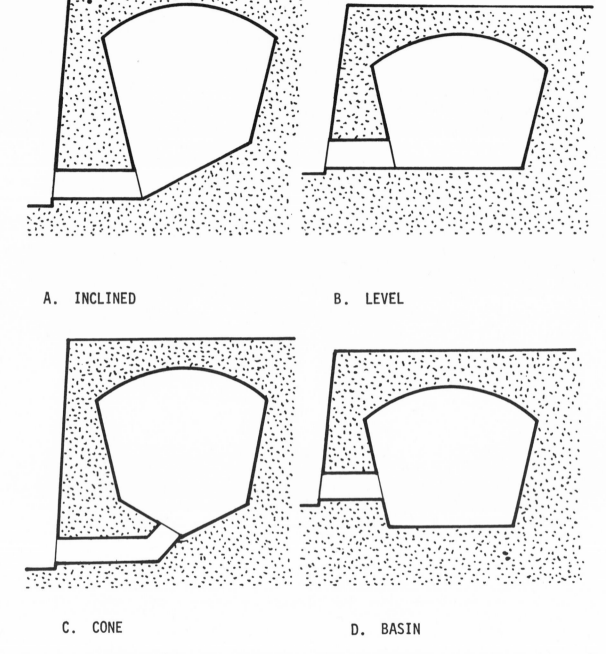

A. INCLINED   B. LEVEL

C. CONE   D. BASIN

Fig. 24. Basic forms and outlets of modern below-ground granaries used in China.

of the tunnel and does not have a wind catcher on top.

The food storage area we surveyed has a 3.2-meter front wall made of natural loess soil that was cut to form the entrance. The width of the storage area is 4.0 meters and its length is 40 meters. The height of the vault is 4 meters. The below-ground diameter of the chimney is 3

meters and the height is more than 8 meters above ground. The height of the cliff to the patio floor is 10 meters.

Ten food storage caves were built in 1967 near Tian Yi village and belong to Liquan County. They are all of the same design and are used to store mostly apples and other fruit. They range from 40 to 43 meters long.

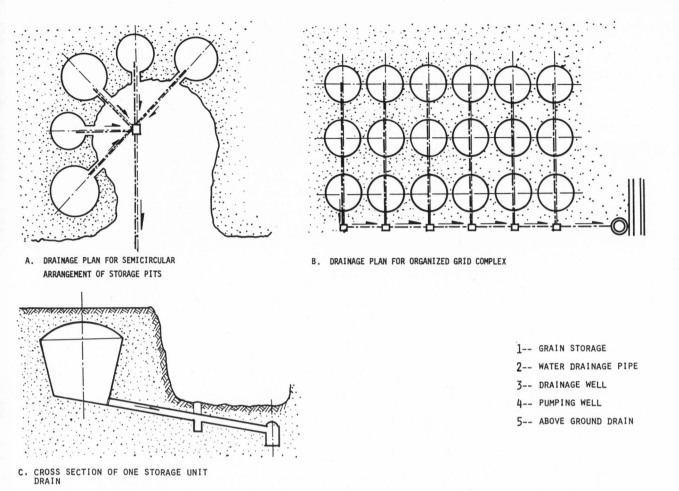

A. DRAINAGE PLAN FOR SEMICIRCULAR
   ARRANGEMENT OF STORAGE PITS

B. DRAINAGE PLAN FOR ORGANIZED GRID COMPLEX

C. CROSS SECTION OF ONE STORAGE UNIT
   DRAIN

1-- GRAIN STORAGE
2-- WATER DRAINAGE PIPE
3-- DRAINAGE WELL
4-- PUMPING WELL
5-- ABOVE GROUND DRAIN

Fig. 25. Design types of modern Chinese below-ground granaries, with consideration of water drainage.

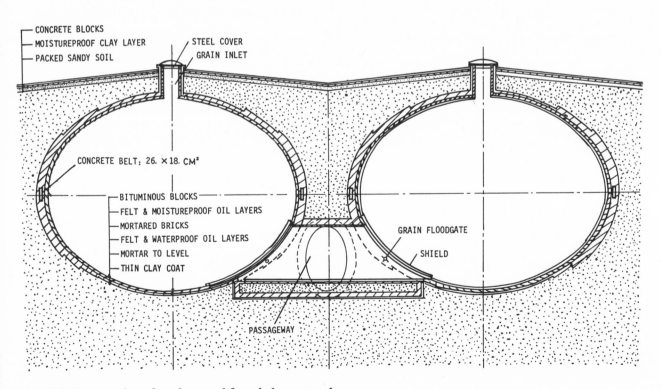

CONCRETE BLOCKS
MOISTUREPROOF CLAY LAYER
PACKED SANDY SOIL
STEEL COVER
GRAIN INLET

CONCRETE BELT: 26. × 18. CM²

BITUMINOUS BLOCKS
FELT & MOISTUREPROOF OIL LAYERS
MORTARED BRICKS
FELT & WATERPROOF OIL LAYERS
MORTAR TO LEVEL
THIN CLAY COAT

GRAIN FLOODGATE
SHIELD

PASSAGEWAY

Fig. 26. Crosssection of modern oval form below-ground granary.

SCALE : 0 1 2 3 4 5M

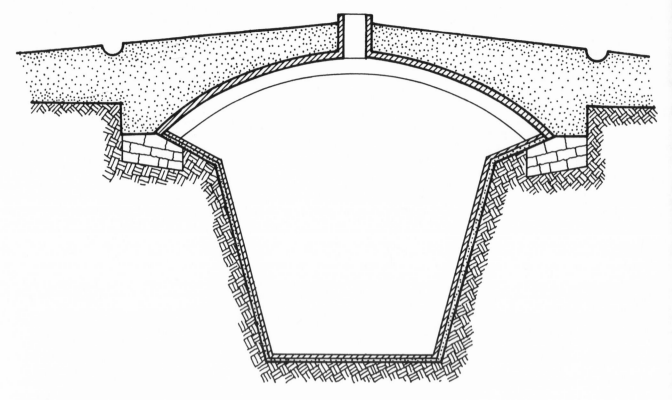

Fig. 27. Modern design of parabolic form of a Chinese below-ground granary.

0   2   4M

COST

According to the Chinese, by 1978 there were 50 million kilograms of grain stored below ground, which equaled a total cost of 12 million yuan ($1.00 = 1.60 yuan). The average construction cost was 12,000 yuan per 50,000 kilograms storage capacity, which constitutes 60 percent of equivalent above-ground granary cost. To construct an underground granary with a capacity of 50 million kilograms of grain, the savings were more than 8 million yuan. Also, the maintenance expenditure for the below-ground granary was very low: 2 yuan per 5,000 kilograms of grain.

An additional economic factor is the wood shortage in China. An underground granary is constructed of bricks and stones and does not need a wooden framework, as do above-ground structures. More than 20,000 cubic meters of timber can be saved in building a below-ground granary for 500 million kilograms of grain. Also, most of the project can be built by common laborers. This is an important factor, especially in rural regions.[13]

BELOW-GROUND URBAN SPACE

China is a densely populated country with more than one city having many million residents. Below-ground space responds positively to the issue of congestion.

In general, the number of dwelling units per acre is quite low in urban China because of the urban sprawl of low apartments and housing. Only recently have high-rise buildings been built in Shanghai, Beijing, and a few other cities. The existing pattern, however, requires a lengthy network of utilities, increased maintenance and construction expenditures, and diverts financial resources from other pressing needs. Moreover, lengthy utility lines detract from the efficiency of the network and reduce its quality. In any case, the utilization of below-ground space brings various land uses into closer proximity and therefore reduces consumption of transportation and exhibits social interaction and effective use of city surfaces. The unique characteristics of Chi-

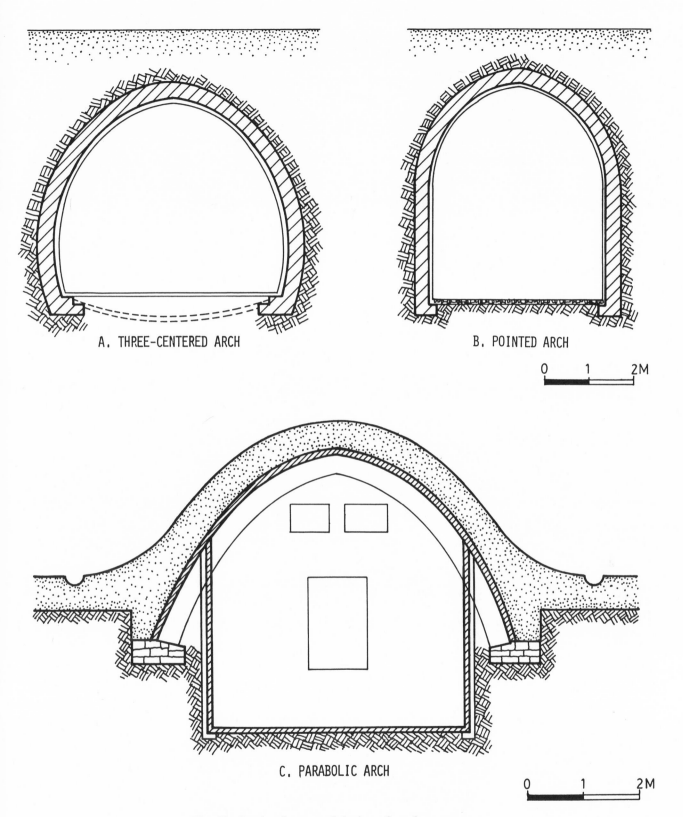

A. THREE-CENTERED ARCH

B. POINTED ARCH

0   1   2M

C. PARABOLIC ARCH

0   1   2M

Fig. 28. Semiunderground design of modern granary.

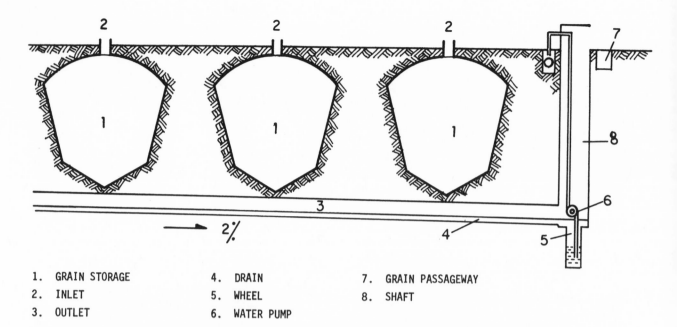

1. GRAIN STORAGE	4. DRAIN	7. GRAIN PASSAGEWAY
2. INLET	5. WHEEL	8. SHAFT
3. OUTLET	6. WATER PUMP	

Fig. 29. Linear type design with one drainage solution for a modern Chinese granary.

Fig. 30. Front entrances to the below-ground food storage facility of Liquan County, Shaanxi Province.

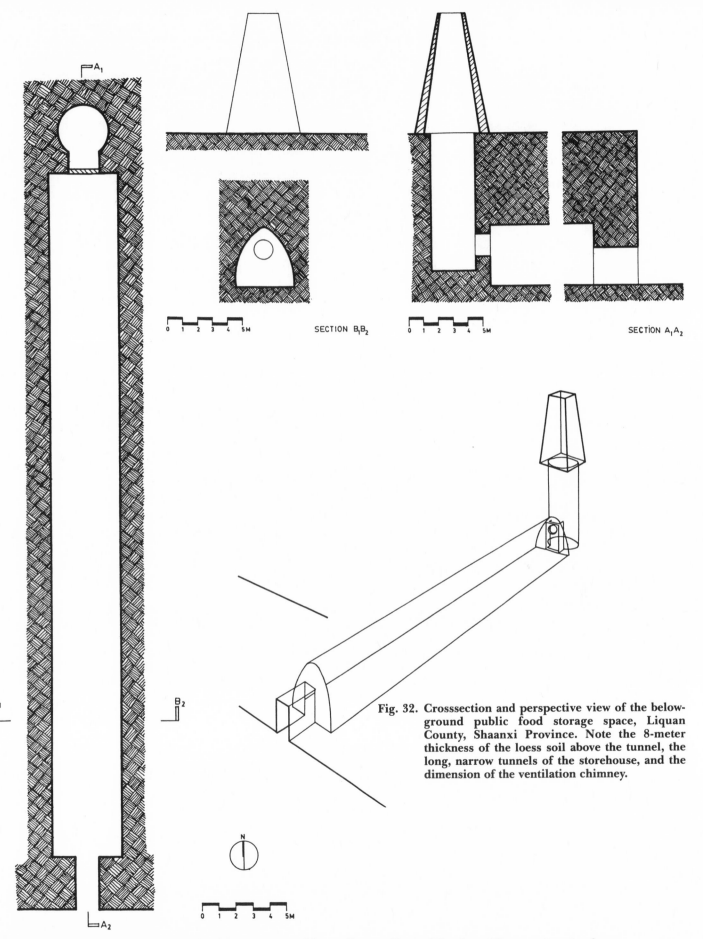

SECTION B₁B₂

SECTION A₁A₂

Fig. 32. Crosssection and perspective view of the below-ground public food storage space, Liquan County, Shaanxi Province. Note the 8-meter thickness of the loess soil above the tunnel, the long, narrow tunnels of the storehouse, and the dimension of the ventilation chimney.

Fig. 31. Plan of below-ground public food storage space, Liquan County, Shaanxi Province. There are ten storehouses like this constructed parallel to each other.

nese society—cohesiveness, informality, friendliness, and pragmatism—seem to belong to a compact city.

THE CHALLENGE

The use of below-ground space in most Chinese cities is primarily nonresidential. It is estimated that more than 50 percent of city land use is for nondwellings. Evidently the Chinese decision to use below-ground space has adopted this basic principle.

In many cities of developed countries nonresidential spaces have been moving slowly yet steadily underground. Such facilities are the windowless types that can be accommodated easily below ground such as restaurants, theaters, libraries, parking garages, storage facilities, shopping centers, refrigeration spaces, and so on.

Space consumption is a major issue in China because of its excessive population (above one billion) and the intensive utilization of land. Moreover, the standard Chinese apartment is small, with only one or two rooms, and lacks guest rooms or a dining room for social gatherings. Therefore, Chinese citizens constantly search outdoor space for entertainment and social interaction. Although many cities provide large central parks, they may be far from residential neighborhoods and do not meet all the needs of the people. City streets are always crowded, as are the shopping centers. Under such conditions, the use of below-ground space for public entertainment becomes an essential and real alternative. In a planned society like China's, building underground has been increasingly used for public gatherings and other purposes in the last three decades, especially in the eighties.

1981 statistics point out that in 236 Chinese cities there are:

one cinema for every 260,000 people;
one multipurpose auditorium for every 540,000 people;
one theater for every 350,000 people;
one public art center for every 600,000 people;
one cultural center for every 1,200,000 people;
one exhibition hall for every 6,600,000;
one public library for every 600,000 people;
one museum for every 850,000 people;

one stadium for every 200,000 people;
one gymnasium for every 1,800,000 people;
one bookstore for every 80,000 people; and
one children's theater for every 500,000 people.[14]

Most of those facilities are located in city centers and are not near outlying neighborhoods.

NONRESIDENTIAL USAGE

In Beijing, almost 80 percent of the primary schools in four districts and 40 percent of the middle schools have no playgrounds. In Huangpu District of Shanghai, which has fifty-three schools, there is only 0.37 square meters of space for each student.[15] The emphasis on industry in large cities has led to a neglect of the needs for social and cultural space. In these cities and others, the only option left is the use of below-ground space for cultural and social activities. The nature of such activities is that they occur only for a short time throughout the day and also produce noise, thereby making them suitable for below-ground space. Other facilities, such as schools, stores, or restaurants, do not need windows and also are occupied only part of the day.

The plan is to use public below-ground space in peacetime as well as during wars. The Chinese consider this multiuse plan an economical as well as an efficient maintenance measure. Public or private nonresidential structures can use below-ground space in many varied ways, as, for example: production, industry and management, entertainment (theater, auditorium, etc.), education (school, library, classroom, sports facility), auto repairs, food supply (restaurant, refrigeration, storage, delivery points), offices, hospitals, shops, exhibition halls, tunnels and passageways, parking garages, transportation arteries, and utilities. In any case, China has been moving reasonably quickly toward the usage of below-ground space for nonresidential dwellings in an urban setting.

UNDERGROUND CHONGQING

For the past forty years the city of Chongqing, Sichuan Province, has become a leader in the use of modern below-ground space because of its lithologically and topographically unique conditions. Below-ground facilities, such as factories, classrooms, warehouses, refrigeration spaces, assembly rooms, laboratories, and teahouses, are now in use in the city.

Chongqing is located 2,000 kilometers upstream on the Yangtze River, at the peninsula triangle created by the meeting of the Yangtze and Jialing Jiang rivers. This triangle is cut by cliffs and gullies on the river sides. The city rises steeply 30 to 50 meters above the rivers, which surround the city on three sides (fig. 33). Sandstone is the primary rock in the city. It is relatively easy to cut and occurs in soft layers. The population density is second only to Shanghai and the city is the largest collector and disperser of goods in southwestern China. In the central district of Chongqing there are 430,000 permanent residents living on the 9.3 square-kilometer peninsula. Thus an average of 12.4 square meters is available per person. At the city's crowded center buildings occupy 85 percent of the space. The need for dwellings has eliminated the last piece of open green space, leaving no areas available for development of new facilities.[16]

In Chinese cities there is no need for land acquisition since all urban land is controlled by the government. In Chongqing the land is rocky and does not require "cut and cover" but uses "cut and use" methods instead. Thus construction time is shorter. There is no need to demolish above-ground buildings in order to create below-ground space, and there is much flexibility in site selection of below-ground space since most of the space is "free" for selection. The city does not have clear zoning. Residential areas were built near factories by the industrial and commuting population to reduce depen-

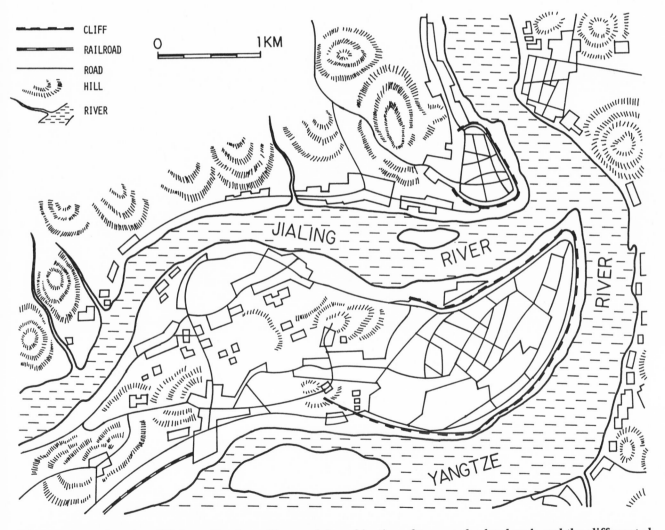

Fig. 33. Chongqing city of Sichuan Province. The special combination of topography, hard rock, and the cliff created by the two rivers give the peninsula a unique feature that supports the usage of below-ground space. Chongqing is one of the warmest cities in China.

dency on transportation. Land for expansion is limited; housing is congested and environmental quality is poor. The possibilities of building new warehouses and industry above ground are almost nil because of the topography of the city. Nor is use as farmland acceptable, either. The possibilities for underground expansion have become realistic and offer hope. For the local officials this option is cheaper than high-rise structures.

The building density of the metropolitan area is 85 percent and is higher in the city. Residential building has been increasing at the rate of more than one million square meters every year, putting more demand on public facilities. Chongqing is one of the "furnaces" of China because of its long, hot summers (between May and September the city averages thirty-eight days annually with temperatures over 35 degrees C, or 95 degrees F.). Such ambient summer temperatures have increased the demand for below-ground teahouses, restaurants, food storage, refrigeration, and other uses. The use of underground space has led to surface preservation and the reduction of air pollution.[17]

Interconnecting tunnels originally had been dug for civil defense but more recently they have been used for other purposes. Some of the excavated rock was used as landfill to enlarge the terraces bordering the two rivers of the city, thus expanding available surface area. In Chongqing subterranean space is used for workshops, electric stations, warehouses, clubrooms, and meeting rooms. More than $200,000 was saved in construction funds by building underground. At a depth of eight meters below ground, the temperature in Chongqing is 18 to 20 degrees C (64.5 to 68 degrees F).[18] The major below-ground facilities in the city include the Sichuan Ship Repair Yard, the workers' facilities at the main Chongqing Bus Terminal, and the Chongqing Watch and Clock Company.

Sichuan Ship Repair Yard. The ship repair plant had very limited possibilities for expansion until 1965. Since then they have dug into the cliff behind the plant and constructed 7,275 square meters of underground floor space, also gaining 30,000 square meters of surface area. Most of this underground construction does not have additional masonry walls. There are general and precision manufacturing plants, a 400-kilowatt power station (which has been operating for ten years), a 1,200-ton water tank, and an auditorium. There is passive and active ventilation, which keeps the humidity at 65–75 percent and the average temperature at 21 degrees C (70 degrees F).[19]

Chongqing Bus Terminal. This large underground project developed at Chongqing is for the employees of the public transportation terminal located in the hub of the city. This rest and relaxation center has tearooms, meetingrooms, a small auditorium comprising 1,260 square meters, and another 2,000 square meters of subsurface space available for expansion.[20]

Chongqing Watch and Clock Company. The third underground project developed in Chongqing city is a watch and clock factory that produces medium-sized clocks, watches, and antishock equipment. This factory, located in the suburbs of the city and surrounded by densely populated farmland, had an urgent need for expansion. The factory has built 8,715 square meters of space below ground for an auditorium, dining hall, kitchen, meetingrooms, and restrooms. Also under construction are workshops, warehouses, storerooms, and electrical generating rooms. In 1981 this space was also expected to house a power station, an underground cinema, a hospital, and food storage cellars.[21]

In cities located in hilly areas like Chongqing, underground space is convenient and drains well. Moreover, the space can be multilevel due to the topography. Construction within the sandstone is easy and low-priced. These factors have led to increased use of below-ground space in the city for such purposes as workshops, storerooms, telecommunication stations, biological research centers, laboratories, auditoriums, meetingrooms, classrooms, tearooms, exhibition halls, cafeterias, restaurants, and many other uses. In some crowded areas of Chongqing and Shanghai, schools use below-ground space.

In Chongqing underground roads are constructed instead of widening the existing hillside roads. This system improves traffic and eliminates changes in land use. Due to Chongqing topographical constraints construction of highway tunnels is locally considered to be cheaper than constructing surface roads. Some units, including Chongqing University, process the rubble gained from underground construction into building stone and sell it to reduce construction costs.[22] In the late 1980s there has been an increase in the use of below-ground space for refrigerating meat and storage of grain, fruit,

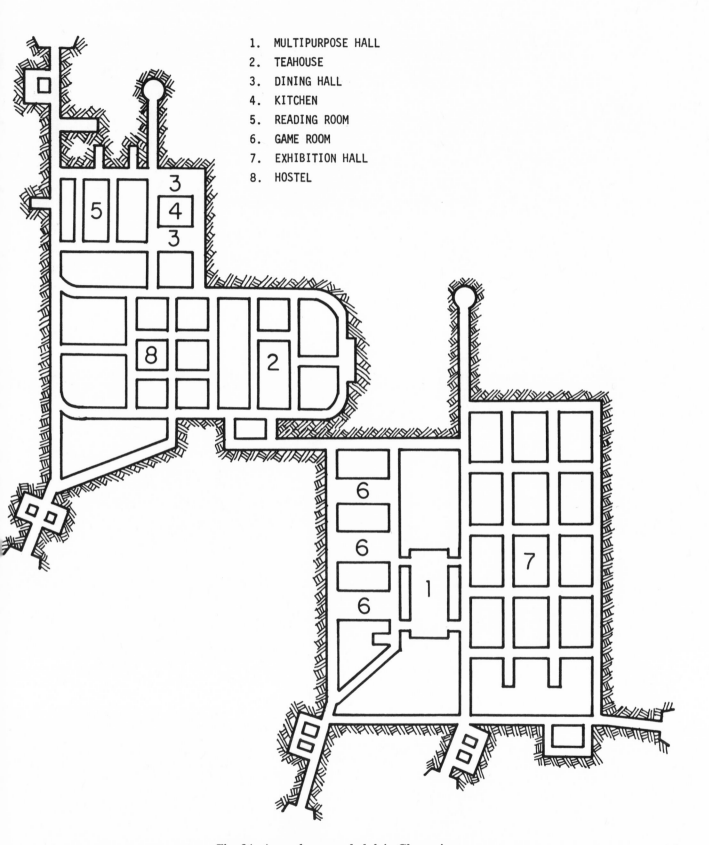

1. MULTIPURPOSE HALL
2. TEAHOUSE
3. DINING HALL
4. KITCHEN
5. READING ROOM
6. GAME ROOM
7. EXHIBITION HALL
8. HOSTEL

Fig. 34. An underground club in Chongqing.

vegetables, chemical products, and miscellaneous goods.

Natural Ventilation. In Chongqing below-ground air is used in summer to cool above-ground structures, especially public buildings such as theaters, stores, offices, and factories. Cool below-ground air currents were first used in 1973. Their usage has lowered the temperature of above-ground buildings 3 to 5 degrees C below the outdoor air temperature. The May First Cinema, whose indoor temperature often reached 36 degrees C (97 degrees F) during the summer, was, in 1975, able to lower the temperature by at least 4 degrees C below the outdoor temperature. The Wide-Screen Cinema has also used the same type of natural ventilation system. Obviously this has saved the cost of air-conditioning. A below-ground natural ventilation system was also introduced to the Chongqing cigarette factory, where steaming, boiling, and roasting tobacco raised the indoor temperature 5 to 6 degrees C higher than the outdoor temperature. The temperature frequently reached an intolerable 40 to 50 degrees C (104 to 122 degrees F) in the summer. Dust accumulation was also a problem. With the introduction of a below-ground 300-meter ventilation duct, the indoor temperature was reduced by 3 to 5 degrees C and the heavy dust was kept down by the cooler air. Similar systems of below-ground air ventilation are also used in textile weaving mills. Recently more and more units in Chongqing have started to use these methods.[23] The Chinese natural ventilation system of directing cool air from below-ground tunnels to above-ground warm structures without using energy has proven to be very successful in Chongqing.

Other Uses. Other examples of below-ground space development in Chongqing include the Chongqing Pharmaceutical Company, the First Textile Mill, and facilities needing ideal conditions of temperature and humidity below-ground in order to store vegetables and grow earthworms and flowers, and "cloud ears" (mushrooms).[24] Suburban Chongqing communities also raise malt and bean sprouts in underground spaces. Moreover, stable below-ground temperatures and humidity enable these factories to produce year round.

According to the planners in Chongqing, chickens that are raised underground in Chengdu city thrive because the temperature is controlled and the light is regulated. Hens produce more eggs and gain weight more rapidly.

In Chongqing there is an underground club for workers (fig. 34). The club has a floor space of 5,000 square meters and includes teahouses, reading rooms, an electronic game room, an exhibition hall for paintings and calligraphy, and other facilities. There is also an underground multipurpose amusement area with theaters, music halls, teahouses, and snack bars (fig. 35). [25]

The Chuangxi Yuan (Sweet Spring Garden) Entertainment Center on Suan Hangzi Street was dug in 1965 and began to be used in 1983, at first as a skating rink and in 1985 as a dance hall (fig. 36). It is more than 10 meters deep and 2 kilometers long. Like other below-ground facilities, it is composed of linear tunnels, parallel or at right angles to each other. The vaults are 7 meters high and some, such as in the dance hall, are 8 meters wide. An entrance fee is charged. When we visited in the evening, the center was crowded with young people, mostly eighteen to twenty-five years old. It has 2,000 square meters now in use and other parts not yet developed. Not every district of the city has a similar entertainment center, and this is the only one in the Saping Ba district. Other below-ground spaces in this district are used for storage, conference rooms, and mushroom raising (fig. 37).

The Golden Bamboo Entertainment Center, Chongqing, was built in 1971 under a high hill as an air defense shelter and was converted to an entertainment center in 1986. It is 27 meters at its deepest point (fig. 38). There are 4,000 square meters, including the corridors, and it can accommodate 1,400 people at one time. The average number of daily visitors is 800. The government spent a little more than one million yuan for the conversion. It has an attractive interior environment and is very well designed and decorated. Although this is the largest below-ground entertainment center in Chongqing, it is rather far from the bulk of the city's population.

The Jiao Tong Hotel cost 1,700,000 yuan to complete and was finished in April 1984. It totals 3,500 square meters. The conference hall is approximately 10 by 25 meters and has 100 seats. The hotel, the entertainment center, and the market (under construction in 1987), are all interconnected.

The Yen Shan Hotel at No. 172 Lanchu Road is 1,700 square meters in area and has three hundred beds. There are rooms containing one, two, or more beds (common), and corridors with

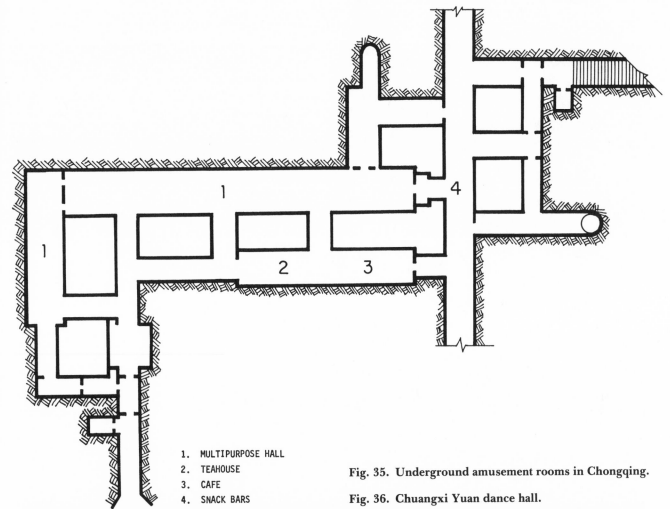

1. MULTIPURPOSE HALL
2. TEAHOUSE
3. CAFE
4. SNACK BARS

Fig. 35. Underground amusement rooms in Chongqing.

Fig. 36. Chuangxi Yuan dance hall.

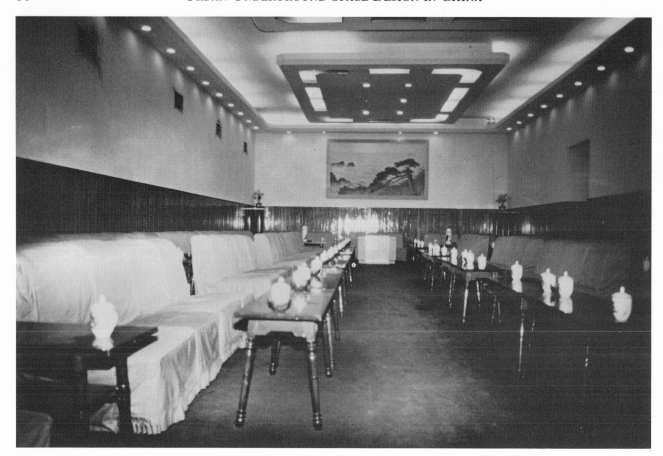

Fig. 37. Conference hall in a hotel.

a mass of attached beds (fig. 39). The facility is essentially a tunnel vault approximately 200 meters long, 3 to 6 meters high, and 3 to 8 meters wide. It was built in 1976 and has been used as a hotel since 1982. Close to the street and near railroad and bus stations, the hotel is on two levels and is connected to a cinema. Three persons who live nearby manage the place. Foreigners cannot be accommodated here.

The Gele Mountains Below-Ground Museum near Chongqing was opened in 1986 in memory of those who died in the 1949 war. According to the Chinese, the Americans had a police station on the opposite mountain during the Communist Revolution and supported the Kuomingtang forces under General Chiang Kai-Shek by providing them information about the Communists. Consequently, large numbers of Chinese were tortured and killed at this place.

The meat refrigeration plant at Dabanqiao opened in 1975 with a storage capacity of 500 tons and a freezing capacity of 12 tons per day.

Of a total of 1,140 square meters of floor space, the underground space comprises 800 square meters. The cost per ton of capacity is $400, which is 26 percent lower than that of equivalent above-ground structures. In addition, there is a reduction in energy consumption when the temperature in the refrigerator remains constant. Since heat exchange in below-ground refrigeration is very low, there is very little temperature fluctuation. There was less than one degree C rise in temperature twenty-four hours after the machines stopped. Ten such refrigeration storage units were constructed throughout the city of Chongqing, yielding a total floor space of 16,600 square meters and storage capacity of over 10,000 tons.[26]

Fruit and Vegetable Storage. Without further preservation, fruit and vegetables can be stored for long periods of time in underground spaces by utilizing the naturally low temperature and high relative humidity. In Chongqing the Depart-

Fig. 38. Entrance to below-ground entertainment center originally designed as an air-raid shelter.

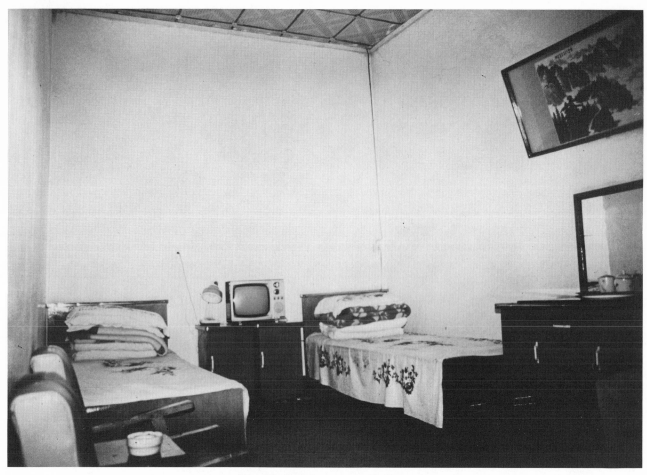

Fig. 39. Hotel accommodations.

ments of Commerce and of Agricultural Research have developed such storage areas. As mentioned before, the Chinese have a long history of experience in storing fruit, vegetables, and grain in below-ground space. Many of the cave dwellings developed in the loess soil in northern China have such facilities. The system retains the freshness of the fruit and vegetables and minimizes dehydration and decay. In this way the system provides products to the market in the off-seasons. Some areas use civil defense shelters for such food storage. For example, the Xiejiawan underground vegetable storage utilized an air raid shelter that could store 200,000 kilograms (200 tons) of vegetables. Jiulongbo Fruit Storage is another underground area that uses a civil defense shelter to store food with good results. For example, only 75.35 percent of the oranges stored above ground for forty-three days remained in good condition while 91.54 percent of the fruit stored below ground for fifty-six days kept their good quality. The De-

partment of Agriculture has also found that oranges can be stored below ground for up to half a year and still retain freshness.[27]

In Chongqing city underground granaries have also had good results by using civil defense shelters. One example is Beichaoyang Underground Granary. The average annual temperature there ranged between 16 to 21 degrees C (61 to 70 degrees F) and the relative humidity between 80–100 percent. To make such space suitable for rice storage, plastic sheeting was laid against the walls, floor, and ceiling to keep out the dampness. Then the opening was sealed with iron-plated wooden doors. After such treatment the temperature within the storage remained at 16 to 20 degrees C (61 to 68 degrees F) and relative humidity at about 66 percent.[28]

Comparison tests were run in the Beichaoyang granary and above-ground storage facilities, using the same methods of packaging and the same amount of grain. The results showed that temperatures above ground fluctuated as the

Fig. 40. Restaurant under Xidan Street.

weather changed, rising to 29 degrees C (84.5 degrees F) when the summer air temperature was at 36 degrees C (97 degrees F), and similarly the grain temperatures rose. Since below-ground temperatures changed little, the grain temperature was also fairly stable, usually below 20 degrees C (68 degrees F). In addition the water content of rice stored underground varied between 12.6 and 13.87 percent, with normal color. Rice stored above ground varied in water content from 12.7 to 14 percent and had lost its color slightly. The test showed greater activity of microorganisms and insects, as well as greater respiration of the grain above ground: for example, a test of carbohydrate activity showed 36 percent more hydroxides in grain stored underground while there was 22 percent more of the original sugar in grain stored above ground. Under constant temperature and humidity the grain below ground was little affected by mold and had a low respiration rate. Accordingly the quality remained high and there was little decrease in dextrose. The test on the rice stored above ground showed insect damage two to three months earlier than in the below-ground rice. For the sake of testing, the above-ground rice was chemically treated twice to control insects, while below-ground rice was sealed after the discovery of insects and the air removed with a vacuum pump, thus controlling the insects. In the underground storage facility, sanitation,

color, and taste of the rice was preserved. In addition, the below-ground storage required less labor.[29]

Other warehouses below-ground in the Chongqing region include storage for gunpowder, gasoline, chemicals, and other flammable or dangerous materials. The sandstone in Chongqing city is easy to seal. Thus, the protection areas are decreased by 50 percent over those required above ground. Except for refrigerated storage, all others require drainage of underground water, reduction of humidity, sealing and ventilation, and strict management. For example during the damp season, entry to or removal of goods from storage should be done during the early morning hours when absolute humidity is relatively low and the difference between outdoor and indoor temperatures is minimal. This minimizes the dampening effect on the inside from outdoor heat.[30]

BELOW-GROUND SPACE IN BEIJING

In Beijing, as well as in some other cities of China, construction of below-ground spaces for civil defense was one of many achievements in the 1960s. By 1981 more than one thousand shelters had been constructed in Beijing alone, totaling 400,000 square meters. These spaces now are being used as hotels, workshops, commercial shops, restaurants, theaters, roller-skat-

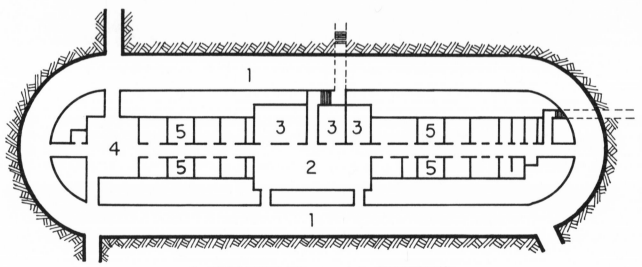

1. ROLLER SKATING RINK   4. RECREATION ROOM
2. LOUNGE   5. GUEST HOUSE
3. ADMINISTRATIVE OFFICE

Fig. 41. Roller skating rink plan in Beijing.

ing rinks, clinics, mushroom-growing facilities, and for other purposes. Already more than one hundred hotels and hospitals with over nine thousand beds are in use. Beijing City Fruit Company can store 3,000 tons of fruit below ground. One-third of Beijing's fruit storage uses below-ground space. Sixty percent of the mushrooms produced in Beijing are raised below ground. For entertainment there are two below-ground theaters built in the 1980s and popular subterranean roller skating rinks that are warm in winter and cool in summer. The use of below-ground space in Beijing has great potential.[31]

On Xidan Street, Beijing, one of the most commercial and crowded shopping streets, there are two new enterprises, the Changan Hotel and the Caveworld Restaurant (fig. 40). The restaurant comprises four dining rooms as well as fast-food and side dish counters. It can accommodate more than two hundred guests. The Changan Hotel is connected with the Caveworld Restaurant. It has sixty-four guest rooms with 320 beds. The two enterprises employ 170 persons. Both the restaurant and the hotel are cooperative enterprises established with the collective capital of the Beijing City Service Company, the West City Foodstuffs Corporation, and the Air Shelter Industries Management Company. Altogether they utilize 4,000 square meters of underground air raid shelters, which equals an eight-story building.

The roller skating rink is under the area of Xidan Street where formerly there was an underground parking lot (fig. 41). It has an oval track 310 meters in circumference and 7.5 meters wide. Sometimes more than four thousand skaters have used it in one day.[32] Another skating rink has been constructed underground in Hanzhou city (fig. 42). The skating rink, which also contains recreation rooms, shops, a tea-house, and a snack bar, is an attractive facility for visitors.

Shopping Center. Qianmen business district is one of the largest and oldest shopping areas in Beijing (fig. 43), yet is is far from satisfactory. In the overall planning of the Qianmen district, an underground shopping space was considered as part of the whole commercial environment (fig. 44). There are only two other major above-ground shopping centers in Beijing: Wangfujing and Xidan streets. Qianmen Street has been a shopping area for the last five hundred years. Its 172 acres are situated in the southern part of the city and run north-south. The proposed plan (introduced in the early 1980s but not yet developed) intends to retain the traditional style,

Fig. 42. Roller skating rink under Gem Mountain in Hangzhou city, Zhejiang Province.

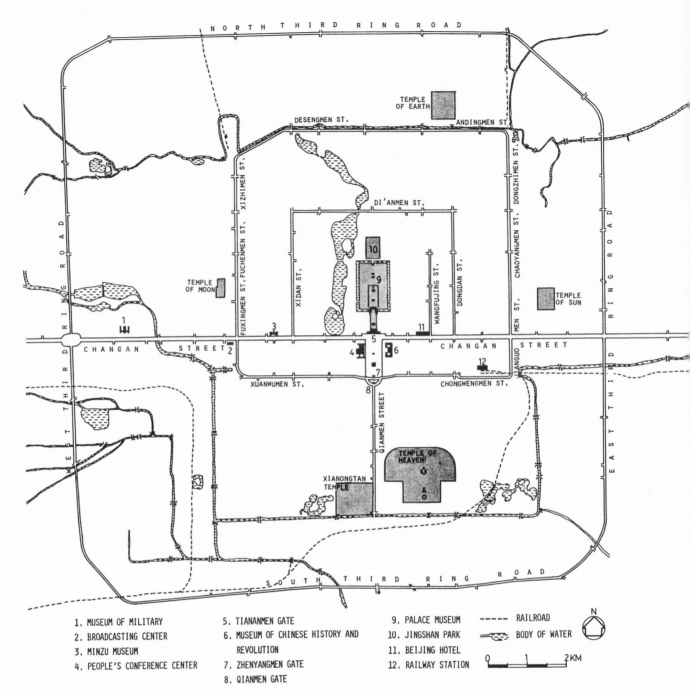

Fig. 43. General plan of Beijing and the location of Qianmen business district (south central part of the map). Note the typical enclosure form of the three concentric roads surrounding the traditional core of the Emperor's Palace and the inner city.

extend the street southward, reform the mass transit, improve the shopping environment, and develop a below-ground shopping center (fig. 45). Qianmen district is extremely overpopulated, having an average of 250,000 people per square kilometer. The district attracts 110,000–

150,000 shoppers per day. The average street width is 20 to 25 meters. More than eight thousand bicycles per hour use the street. The sidewalk is about 2 meters wide with six thousand people per hour passing through. There is no open space for relaxation and the shopping and

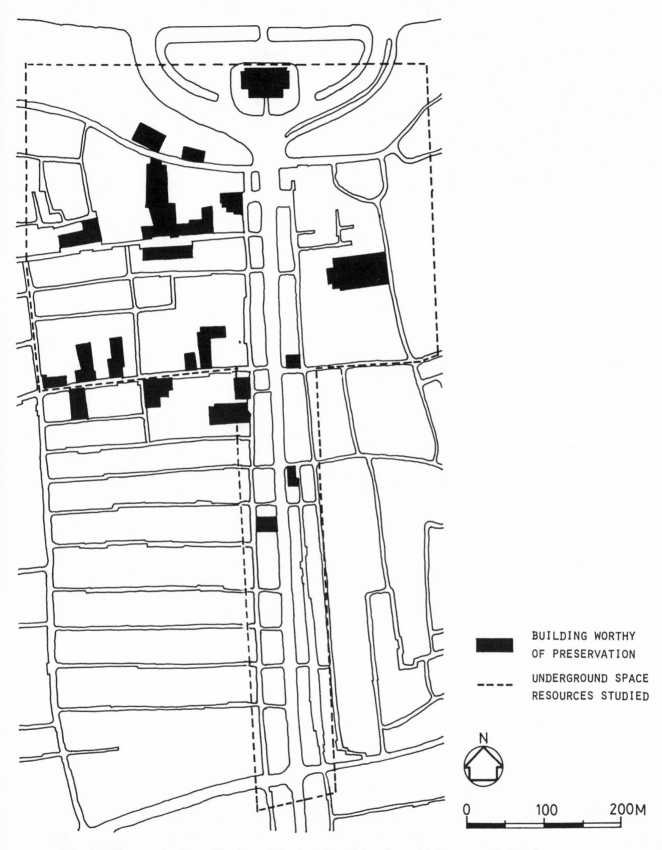

BUILDING WORTHY OF PRESERVATION

- - - **UNDERGROUND SPACE RESOURCES STUDIED**

N

0   100   200M

Fig. 44. Qianmen business district and the location of the planned below-ground shopping center.

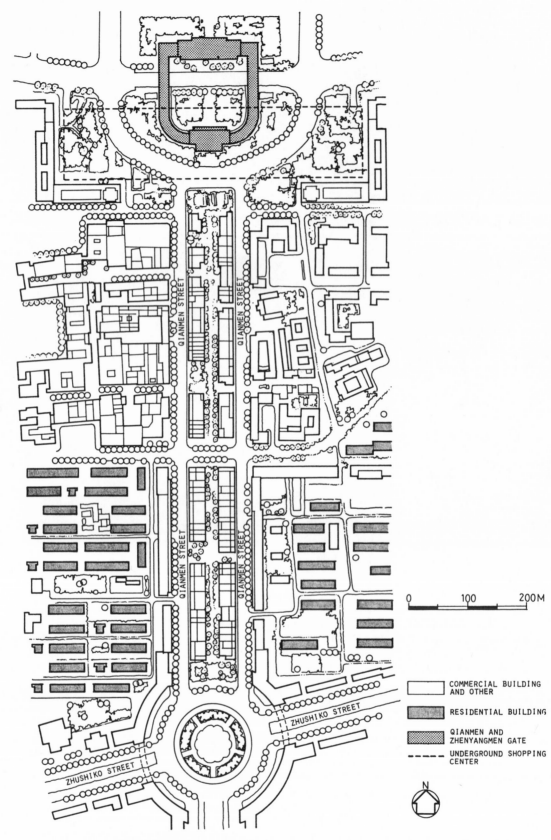

QIANMEN STREET

QIANMEN STREET

QIANMEN STREET

QIANMEN STREET

ZHUSHIKO STREET

ZHUSHIKO STREET

0   100   200M

COMMERCIAL BUILDING
AND OTHER

RESIDENTIAL BUILDING

QIANMEN AND
ZHENYANGMEN GATE

UNDERGROUND SHOPPING
CENTER

N

Fig. 45. Scheme of the general redevelopment of Qianmen business district introduced by Professor Tung and Mr. Jing of Tsinghua University, Beijing.

living environments are of poor quality. Expansion of the shopping space is not feasible unless buildings are demolished and high-rise structures are built, thus eliminating the traditional style. Geologically there is a topsoil layer of 1 to 3 meters with a deep sandy layer below it; the water table is 10 to 15 feet down. There are some shallow subsurface utilities. A maximum depth of fifteen meters can be considered for the underground shopping center, using the "cut and cover" method. The total volume to be used is 3 million cubic meters. The total floor area will be 600,000 square meters on three levels. Considering that five new shopping centers are being speculated for development in Beijing during the 1980s, it is expected that the underground shopping center will increase the purchasing power but actually reduce the number of shoppers in Qianmen Street. Based on these resources, the principles of the underground shopping center are (fig. 46):

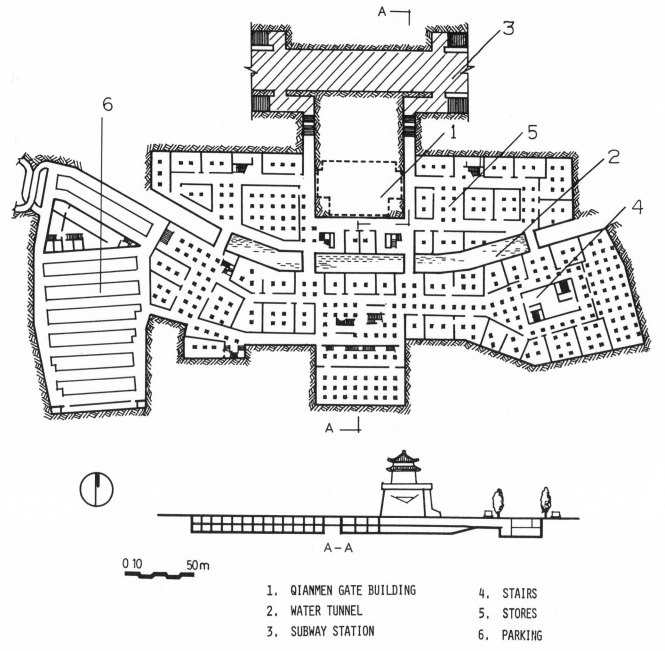

0 10   50m

1. QIANMEN GATE BUILDING
2. WATER TUNNEL
3. SUBWAY STATION
4. STAIRS
5. STORES
6. PARKING

Fig. 46. Schematic plan of Qianmen below-ground shopping area, as presented by Professor Tung and Mr. Jing of Tsinghua University, Beijing.

1. The commerce is to be close to the underground rapid transit system;
2. The complex of services will include restaurants, parking, stores, and subway station;
3. The center will be an organic part of the entire commercial and above-ground section;
4. It will provide relaxation space;
5. The project will develop in stages;
6. The old architecture style of the above-ground buildings will be retained.

The architects view the project as benefiting social, environmental, and economic conditions. Maintenance costs of the below-ground facilities are usually lower than above-ground costs and a "life-cycle cost" is to be considered.[33]

The below-ground Qianmen project was constructed by the government and was started in 1969 as a civil defense center. There are levels at 8, 13, and 15 meters with shops, storage space, a one-hundred bed hotel (originally a medical clinic), and conference rooms (fig. 47). The total length of the interconnected network of tunnels is 3,000 meters, which can accommodate ten thousand people when used as a civil defense facility in wartime. The complex has a generator, a well, communication system, and air filters. At present some eighty thousand people per day visit the shopping center above in To Sa La Street. It takes five to ten minutes to descend to the below-ground complex.

The entire Qianmen civil defense complex is connected to other below-ground projects in Beijing. There is an underground walkway (taking three hours) to the suburbs of Beijing—more than 5 kilometers away. Such an underground complex and network of routes exists in each neighborhood and is connected to every industrial plant in the city proper. The present design policy mandates that all public buildings must have a section below ground as well as ones above. Beijing city proper, with a population of

Fig. 47. Conference room in Qianmen, Beijing, underground network, originally designed for civil defense.

Fig. 48. Subway station in Beijing.

some nine million, can accommodate five million people below ground in case of war. All the below-ground networks are connected and lead to the mountains outside the city to provide mass evacuation in case of disaster.

Beijing Subway. In 1965 the first section (24 kilometers) of the Beijing subway was completed. This part includes seventeen stations at average intervals of 1.5 kilometers (fig. 48). "Cut and cover" construction was possible because of the great width of the streets under which the subway is constructed.

The maximum depth to the ceiling is 10 meters but for the most part the depth between the stations is 2 to 3 meters. The crosssection of tunnel is rectangular, of reinforced concrete, 4.35 meters high and 4.1 meters wide. The stations are finished in marble and the air-conditioned cars are clean and comfortable and are manufactured in China. Each car accommodates 186 people with seats for 60 passengers. They travel at a speed of 80 kilometers per hour. Ultimately 45,000 passengers per hour will be transported in each direction. An additional 57

kilometers of subway tunneling is planned, of which 16.4 kilometers was nearly finished in 1982.[34]

A subway is also being designed for Shanghai. The water table in the city is very high in some places, only one meter below the surface. The soil is soft alluvial deposit. Recently the Chinese have become experienced in shield tunneling, which would be suitable for the Shanghai area. The remarkable Chinese record of tunneling accomplishments is part of their historical achievement in the usage of below-ground space for living, storage, and other common activities. Their building construction pragmatism has embraced this field as well. Moreover, the combination of past practice with modern technology will undoubtedly lead to even greater accomplishments in this field.

Other Uses. In Beijing, as in many other cities, there is an underground cultural center (fig. 49). Beijing's includes an exercise hall, reading room, and television room.[35]

Underground parking is becoming more and more common in China. Usually it is combined

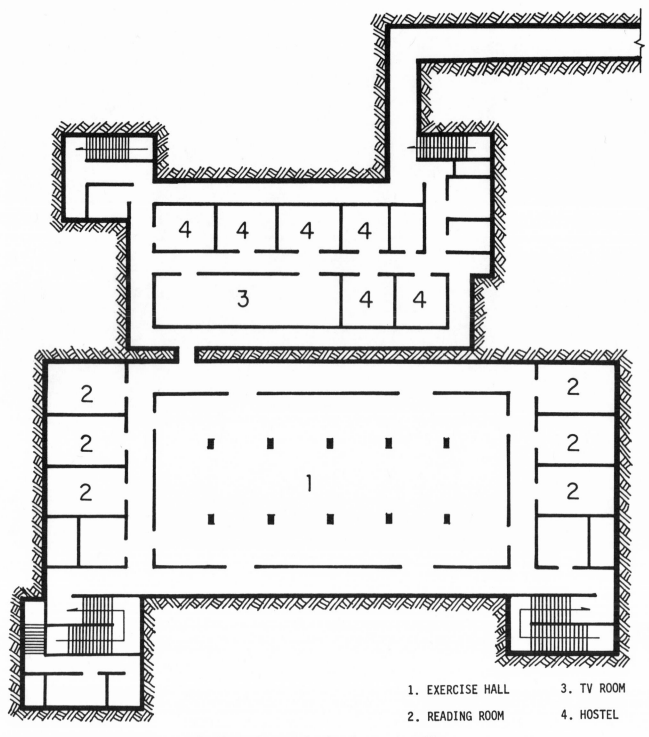

1. EXERCISE HALL   3. TV ROOM

2. READING ROOM   4. HOSTEL

Fig. 49. Underground cultural center in Beijing.

with above-ground shopping. Figure 50 depicts a four-level parking space with markets above ground in Beijing. The parking area holds six hundred vehicles and connects with the subway station.[36]

The Underground Cinema at Hui Bai Tree Street in the Xue Wu district of Beijing was opened for the use of the military in July 1981 in a space originally constructed for civil defense. Planned in 1970, the project consists of a 1,290-

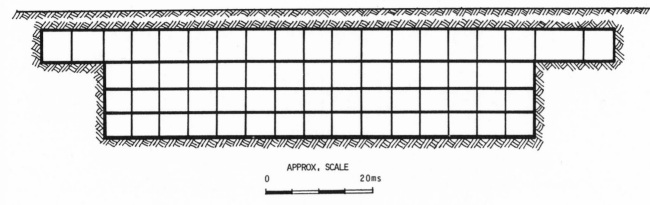

APPROX. SCALE

0   20ms

Fig. 50. Underground parking space with four floors, Shanghai.

seat auditorium and three lounges, with a total area of 4,400 square meters. The lounges are 10 meters below the surface (including the 4 meters floor-to-ceiling height). A deeper part contains the cinema hall, which is 20 meters from floor to surface. The new hill surmounting the cinema contains green parkland. There is no similar place under construction in the mid-1980s in Beijing. The entire complex can hold more than 3,000 people in an emergency. Five or six shows are given daily, sometimes seven in summer. Although the cinema is usually only about half full, it is of course used more at night than in the daytime.

According to the managers, the main problems with the Underground Cinema are overhead earth pressure, which pushes the side walls outward, and the high relative humidity and consequent high condensation. The worst months are June, July, and August, when it is too cold because of the humidity in the air. In winter the cinema is warm and dry. Although there is active ventilation, much odor persists, especially in summer. Some employees complain about the humidity and are compensated with higher salaries.

BELOW-GROUND MODERN FACILITIES

Modern Chinese below-ground facilities have become diversified in their functions and are primarily concentrated in large cities such as Beijing, Shanghai, Chongqing, and Nanjing. As stated earlier, some of these facilities use underground space developed in the past for civil defense.

EDUCATIONAL AND CULTURAL FACILITIES

The Chinese also use below-ground space for education. One university constructed a multi-purpose facility that included a library (fig. 51). The construction of educational and cultural facilities below ground has become common in most large Chinese cities, along with entertainment centers intended for younger age groups (fig. 52).

Hangzhou, or West Lake city, is considered one of the most beautiful Chinese cities. It is located some 150 kilometers southwest of Shanghai and can be reached by train. The city is built in a half-circle around a large mountain lake. Consequently the city intensively used below-ground space by digging into the mountains for a theater, restaurant, dance hall, and other purposes (fig. 53).

The underground theater in Hangzhou is located in the mountain at the northern end of the lake (fig. 54). A long and very wide underground cave contains a theater (86 meters long, 24 meters wide, and 18 meters high) and a large dance hall. The theater seats 1,800 and includes an auditorium, stage, dressing room, projection room, and meeting room (fig. 55 and 56). It has satisfactory lighting, ventilation, acoustics, and air-conditioning. In Hefei, Anhui Province, in eastern China, an underground reading room includes a teahouse, gamerooms, and other facilities (fig. 57). Suzhou, the Garden City, has an underground exhibition hall (fig. 58). The underground auditorium in Harbin, Heilongjian Province, consists of 1,200 seats, projection room, foyer, machine room, workshop, and

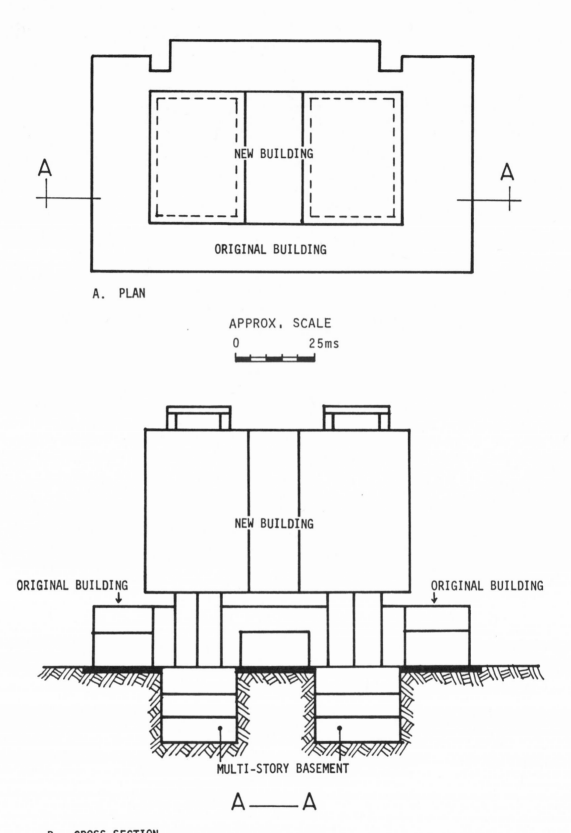

A. PLAN

APPROX. SCALE

0   25ms

NEW BUILDING

ORIGINAL BUILDING   ORIGINAL BUILDING

NEW BUILDING

MULTI-STORY BASEMENT

A——A

B. CROSS SECTION

Fig. 51. High-rise university building with below-ground floors for diverse purposes including a library, Shanghai.

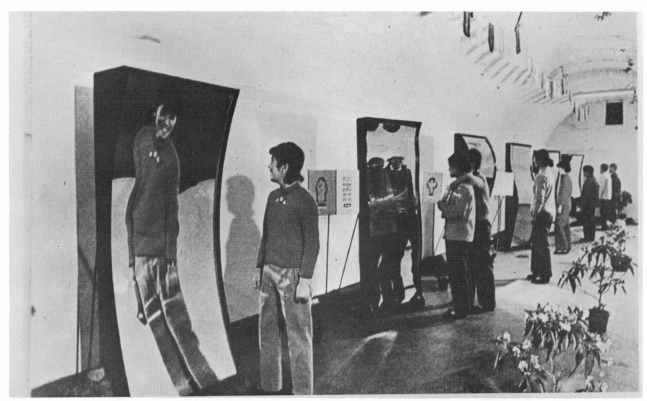

Fig. 52. An entertainment center under Huishan Mountain in Wuxi city, Jiangsu Province.

Fig. 53. Below-ground dance hall in Hangzhou city, Zhejiang Province.

Fig. 54. Underground theater in Hangzhou.

other facilities (fig. 59). Its total floor area is 2,000 square meters.[37]

ACCOMMODATIONS

Hotels below ground have become common, especially in large cities. Because of its beauty Hangzhou (West Lake city) attracts many tourists and has a below-ground hotel with several hundred beds (figs. 60–61). Beijing and other cities have also constructed below-ground hotels (fig. 62).

The special Scenic Spot Restaurant is located near the Yellow River some 40 kilometers northwest of Zhengzhou city, Henan Province. The restaurant is part of a recreation complex called The Scenic Spot of the Yellow River. This area includes a few pavilions and pagodas located at the top of some hills surrounding a small basin and overlooking the nearby huge Yellow River. Long stairways lead to and between each pagoda. At the lower end is a beautiful statue of "Mother Yellow River" breast-feeding her

child—China. Two bridges cross the river at this point (one for railroads and the other for automobiles). In the lower basin gardening and natural beautification is abundant.

The restaurant was built in 1970 to accommodate a large number of people (fig. 63). It forms a tunnel under a hill with the entrance and exit built into two cliffs on opposite sides of the hill. It has two attractive, facing entrances (fig. 64), one of which overlooks the Yellow River, although the view is blocked by a fence (fig. 65). The entrances are decorated with colorful glass and windows in the Chinese tradition. The well-lit main dining room of the restaurant is open to both sides with huge windows. The restaurant director informed us that the average temperature is a comfortable 20 degrees C (68 degrees F) in the summertime and 10 degrees C (50 degrees F) in the winter. The director also said that in addition to its advantages of comfort, the building saved a lot of money in construction because the cost of building materials was less. He mentioned that "high buildings for such pur-

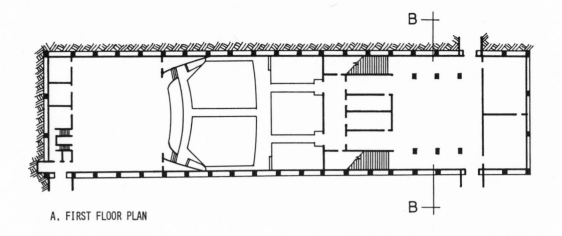

A. FIRST FLOOR PLAN

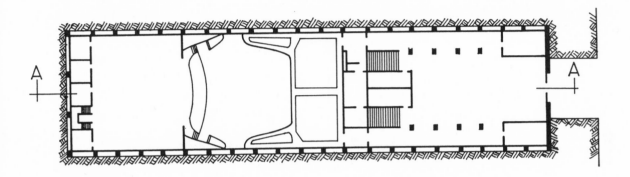

B. SECOND FLOOR PLAN

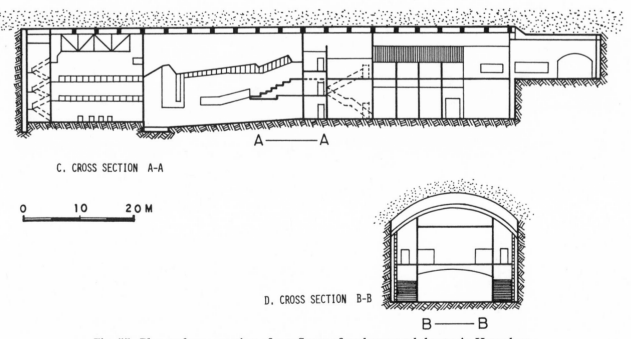

C. CROSS SECTION A-A

A——A

0   10   20 M

D. CROSS SECTION B-B

B——B

Fig. 55. Plan and crosssection of two floors of underground theater in Hangzhou.

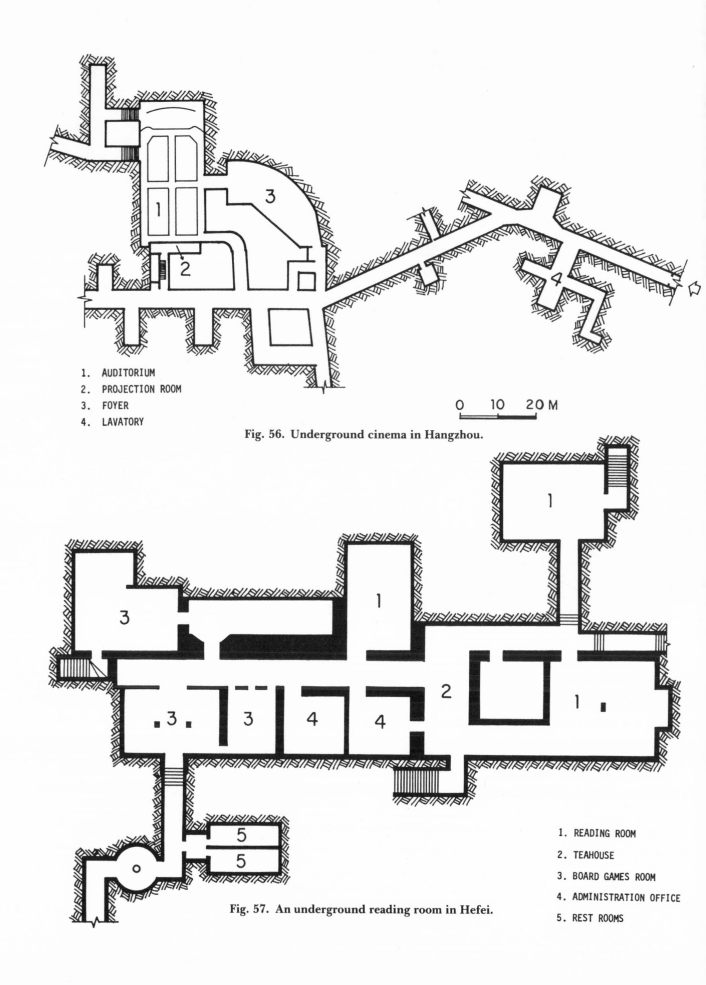

1. AUDITORIUM
2. PROJECTION ROOM
3. FOYER
4. LAVATORY

0 10 20 M

Fig. 56. Underground cinema in Hangzhou.

1. READING ROOM
2. TEAHOUSE
3. BOARD GAMES ROOM
4. ADMINISTRATION OFFICE
5. REST ROOMS

Fig. 57. An underground reading room in Hefei.

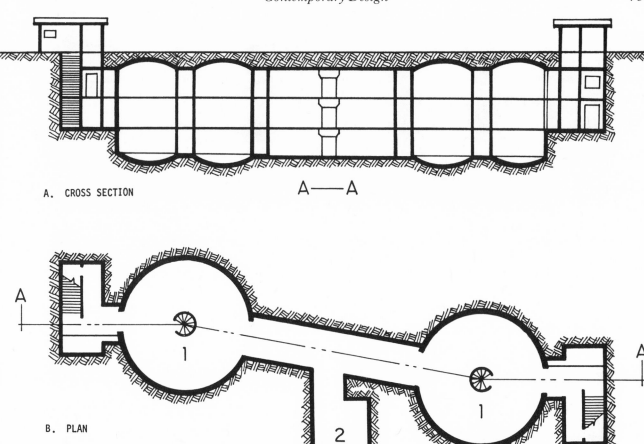

A. CROSS SECTION

A——A

B. PLAN

1. EXHIBITION HALL 2. ELEVATORS

Fig. 58. An underground exhibition hall in Suzhou.

poses may cost 10,000 yuan and this one cost only 1,000 yaun." Restaurants like this were constructed in many other places in China (fig. 66).

TUNNELING

Contemporary tunneling is used extensively in China, especially during the three and a half decades since the establishment of the People's Republic. Thousands of kilometers of tunnels are used for railroads (the most commonly used mode of transportation), subways, roads, water supply, civil defense shelters, and other uses.

Much of Chinese tunneling is accomplished by manual labor. However, mechanical help, using western technology, has increased over the last two decades. Between 1950 and 1979, 1,897 kilometers of railroad tunnels were constructed, which constitutes about 6 percent of the recently constructed rail lines. On six lines tunnels comprise more than 20 percent of the length. Some tunnels are more than 5 kilometers long. Many of the tunnels were in the relatively soft loess soil although in the 1970s and 1980s there has been an increase in rock-cutting as well.[38] The increase in tunneling in China is especially due to the extension of the railway to the mountainous regions. In the 1980s the Chinese began construction of a new railway from Chengdu city (Sichuan Province), 500 meters above sea level, to Lhasa (Tibet), which is 6,000 meters above sea level. This project also requires much tunneling.

In 1972 an underground electric power plant was completed in Shanghai (fig. 67). In September 1970 a subaqueous vehicular tunnel was constructed under the Huang Pu River. It is 2,793 meters long and 10.20 meters in external diameter. Around eight hundred vehicles drive through it daily.[39]

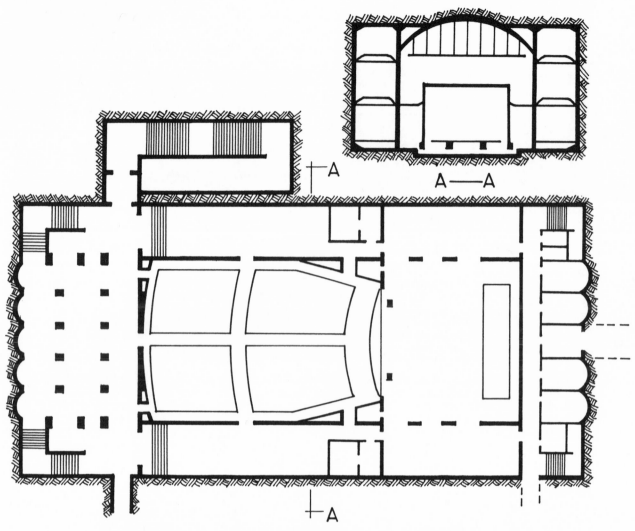

Fig. 59. An underground multipurpose auditorium in Harbin.

Fig. 60. Below-ground hotel room in Hangzhou (West Lake city), Zhejiang Province.

Fig. 61. Corridor in the below-ground hotel in Hangzhou (West Lake city), Zhejiang Province.

Fig. 62. Underground hotel with four hundred beds, Shanghai, intended to be used as a hospital in wartime.

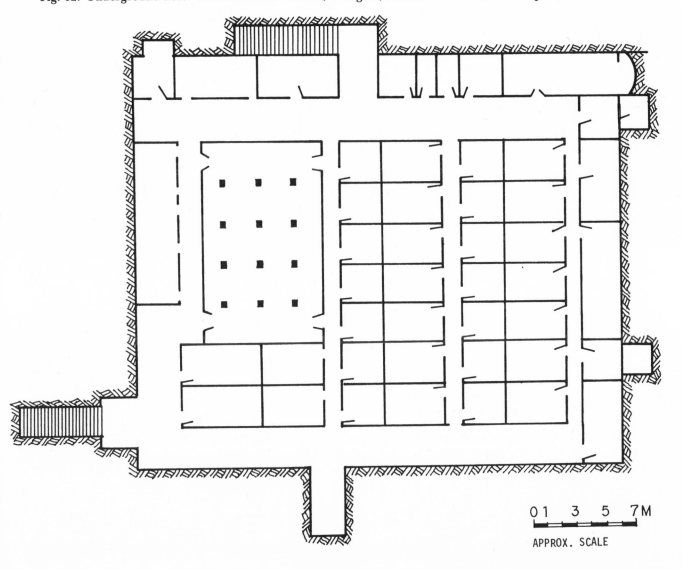

0 1   3   5   7M

APPROX. SCALE

Fig. 63. The front of the below-ground restaurant at the Yellow River Scenic Spot.

Fig. 64. Dining room inside the below-ground restaurant at the Yellow River Scenic Spot.

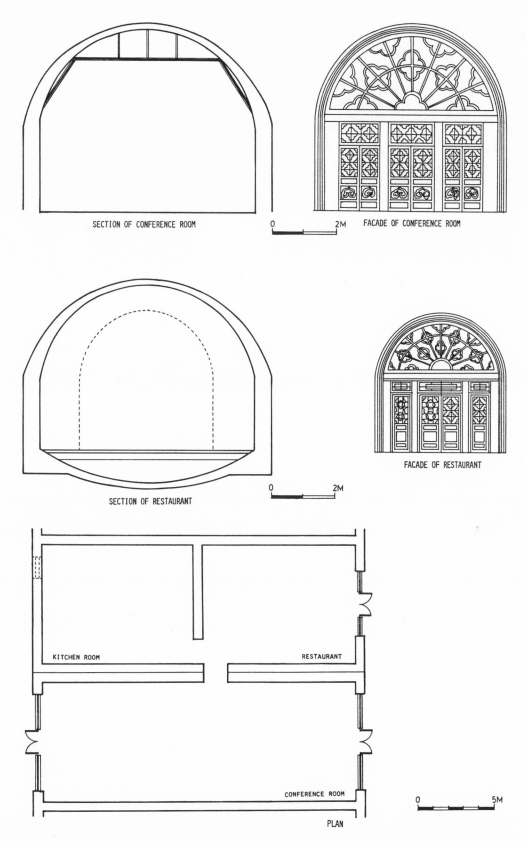

SECTION OF CONFERENCE ROOM

0   2M

FACADE OF CONFERENCE ROOM

SECTION OF RESTAURANT

0   2M

FACADE OF RESTAURANT

KITCHEN ROOM

RESTAURANT

CONFERENCE ROOM

0   5M

PLAN

Fig. 65. Facades and plan of modern restaurant at the Yellow River Scenic Spot, some thirty miles northwest of Zhengzhou city.

Fig. 66. An underground cafe on Xihu Lake, Hangzhou city, Zhejiang Province.

CIVIL DEFENSE SHELTERS

The Chinese plan civil defense facilities as an integral part of the overall urban planning scheme. This policy was formulated in the 1960s, when tension was high between China and the U.S.S.R. Some civil defense shelters were planned to use abandoned mines, the underground transportation space network, or new shelters. The design of civil defense shelters included connecting flat as well as mountainous regions. Thus, under air-raid conditions, people would move from the shelters of the flat area to shelters in the mountains through an underground network. The ultimate goal was that most civil defense shelters of a city would be connected at different levels. Mountain shelters would have effective ventilation and good drainage; however, such systems would need special designs to protect them from air raids.

China's geopolitical situation in the 1960s and its high population density motivated the country to consider civil defense as a high priority. Almost every urban neighborhood has voluntarily constructed a public underground shelter without outside supervision or enforcement of

any common code. It is widely accepted that an underground shelter with a 1-meter earthcover can withstand a nuclear blast occurring two to five miles away. Withstanding a nuclear strike is not simply a matter of design. The neighborhood below-ground shelter can accommodate a few to several hundred people. The shelter consists of large rooms linked together by vaulted tunnels that are approximately 1.37 meters wide, 2.13 meters high, and are covered with 9.14 meters of earth or rock. Food preparation takes place in the larger chamber, with another small space for dining. The shelters are constructed by self-organized associations of the urban neighborhood or district.

Larger and more sophisticated below-ground shelters are built by working units, such as factories, that have mutual interests. The shelter depth is usually 30 meters below ground. They are made of many types of interconnected tunnels of different sizes (fig. 68). The smaller tunnels are used for storage and living space, and are designed to accommodate 30,000 people. The larger tunnels are about 7.62 meters in diameter, are without columns, and are vaulted.

A third type of shelter is larger than the others

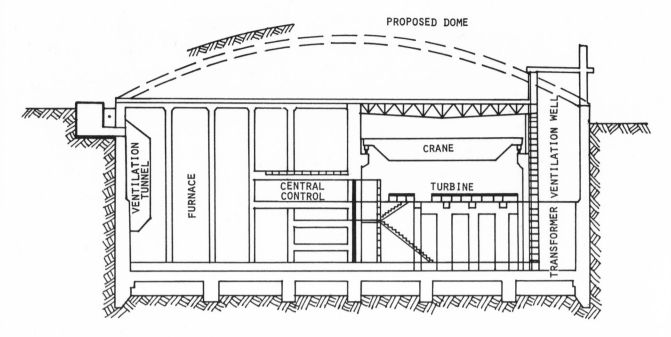

PROPOSED DOME

VENTILATION TUNNEL

FURNACE

CENTRAL CONTROL

CRANE

TURBINE

TRANSFORMER VENTILATION WELL

Fig. 67. Underground electric power generator plant completed in 1972 in Shanghai.

0   5   10 M

Fig. 68. Underground civil defense tunnel in Beijing, 30 meters deep. The tunnel connects different halls of the shelter.

Fig. 69. Below-ground conference room in Beijing, originally constructed for civil defense during the Sino-Russian tension in the 1960s. Large numbers of such rooms have been converted to other uses in the major cities.

and is designed to be used for both defense and daily needs (fig. 69) such as hospitals, recreation centers, hotels, cafeterias, or factories.

Chinese below-ground shelters are lighted by electricity and also supplied with candles. They may also be heated by steam. All have acceptable water facilities and some form of sanitation with sewer and drainage. The ventilation system is generally quite effective. As is common in China, most of the shelters are constructed by manual labor. Tunnels in these below-ground shelters are vast and many are interconnected. They offer mobility and communication advantages, especially for the masses. In the event of a nuclear attack the network would enable evacuation of children and women to the surrounding countryside (fig. 70). In any case, this underground network of tunnels is a massive, independent method of population defense.

Eighty percent of the Chinese population still lives in rural areas. Moreover, any urban survivors from a nuclear strike will need to reach the rural areas. In many rural regions, populations have used or are using below-ground space. These rural people, however, have a better chance of survival because of their dispersion throughout the country. The American concept of civil defense against nuclear strike is based on mass evacuation and early warning. The Chinese concept, on the other hand, is based on an underground network of shelters similar to that of western Europe; in this way they combine their system with the high technology of the West.[40]

COST OF BELOW-GROUND URBAN SPACE

Our research on the use of below-ground space within the loess soil zone for dwellings, as well as for diversified facilities, points out that the construction cost is lower than that needed for comparable above-ground residences of the same size. This lower cost is due to the dual use

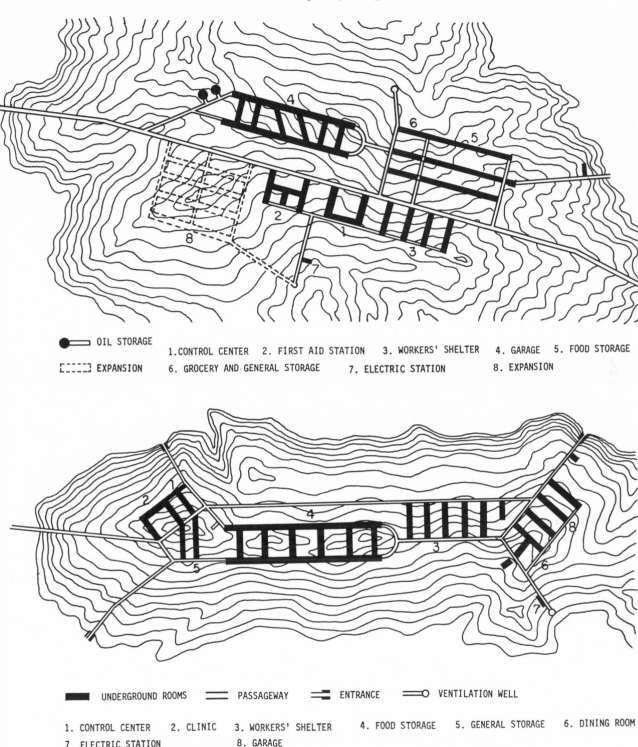

OIL STORAGE   1. CONTROL CENTER   2. FIRST AID STATION   3. WORKERS' SHELTER   4. GARAGE   5. FOOD STORAGE

EXPANSION   6. GROCERY AND GENERAL STORAGE   7. ELECTRIC STATION   8. EXPANSION

UNDERGROUND ROOMS   PASSAGEWAY   ENTRANCE   VENTILATION WELL

1. CONTROL CENTER   2. CLINIC   3. WORKERS' SHELTER   4. FOOD STORAGE   5. GENERAL STORAGE   6. DINING ROOM

7. ELECTRIC STATION   8. GARAGE

Fig. 70. Plans of two types of civil defense shelters in the mountains.

of the land or land preservation, convenience of digging, the need for minimal building materials, the low technology necessary and low maintenance expenditures. The case outside the loess soil zone can differ from place to place and is primarily determined by the type of soil or rocks to be cut. In general the cost is lower than that of above-ground facilities, particularly in congested areas where land value is high and availability of land for expansion is scarce. In comparing the cost of the below-ground structure with an equal above-ground structure, one should consider the life-cycle cost of each one, which is the energy savings and the maintenance cost during the lifetime of the below-ground structure. In any case, the traditional and contemporary use of below-ground space in China has been primarily within the loess soil zone.

3
Thermal Performance

One of the most basic benefits of the construction of below-ground space is the thermal performance introduced by the soil mass, which provides cool ambient temperature in the summer and warmth in the winter. Therefore one needs to become familiar with the thermal performance system of the earth itself in order to achieve optimal design benefits.

HEAT GAIN AND HEAT LOSS

Two basic concepts related to the earth's performance should be understood. One, the earth functions as a thermal insulator between the outdoor and the indoor environments. Second, the soil functions as a heat retainer and processor between different seasons.

The earth is an excellent insulator. In fact, the diurnal influence of the solar radiation on the earth is limited to 7 to 10 centimeters, a limited influence that depends much on the composition of the soil (chemical and physical) and on the level of humidity within the soil. In any case the most intense thermal influence takes place in the afternoon hours between 2:00 to 4:00 P.M. Then the earth's heat begins to diffuse into the air and continues into evening, reaching maximum diffusion just before sunrise, when a new thermal cycle begins.

The thermal retainment in the earth is the main concern in the design of an earth-sheltered structure. Although the solar diurnal radiation influence is limited in depth, there is a slow, steady thermal wave movement into the earth every day to a depth of about 10 meters. It takes one solar season to complete the cycle. Thus, at the depth of 10 meters below ground, the summer outdoor temperature will reach the building by the winter and the winter outdoor temperatures will reach it by the summer. The thermal changes within the building result from the seasonal thermal cycle rather than from the diurnal cycle. Basically, the seasonal influence of the outdoor temperature is limited to 10 to 12 meters below ground. On the other hand, at a deeper level in the earth the temperature will increase because of the geothermal influence. Two major conclusions can be drawn.

1. The below-ground space's diurnal temperature becomes stable during a given season while the outdoor temperature fluctuates diurnally and seasonally. This rule applies to relative humidity as well. An understanding of this important fact is necessary for the proper design of below-ground space for various uses, whether it be for refrigeration, educational facilities, food storage, or other purposes.

2. The depth of the building in the earth (from 0–10 meters) determines the degree of seasonal fluctuation of the indoor temperature. The basic rule is that the deeper

the building underground the more stable the temperature, and vice versa. Thus, refrigeration would be best placed at a depth of 10 meters in order to save energy. Heat loss also depends to some degree on the physical and chemical composition of the soil, as well as on its degree of relative humidity.

One basic question arises from this discussion. Must we put the structure at a depth of 10 meters in order to obtain a seasonal stable temperature or can we obtain such stability at less depth? It is possible to put the building at a depth of less than 10 meters and still obtain similar results by covering the earth with trees, shrubs, or above-ground buildings that interfere with heat sinking into the ground. In fact, our ancestors understood the thermal performance of the earth quite well by observation and practice. In the Middle East, however, they developed thick retaining walls in above-ground buildings that provide similar, but not identical, amounts of coolness in the summer and warmth in the winter. Such structures in the city of Jerusalem, for example, were built with thick walls: 1 to 1½ meters of earth were sandwiched between two retaining walls of stone. In the Mediterranean climate (cool and wet in winter and warm and dry in the summer), humidity and coolness absorbed by the outer walls during the winter moves toward the interior and reaches it by the summer. A similar process occurs in the summer when the outdoor walls receive the maximum temperatures, which arrive in the interior by the winter and radiate heat to the interior space.

The above description of the thermal process within the earth is very basic, yet each site has its own unique characteristics, which result from a variety of factors such as site orientation in relation to the movement of the sun, soil composition, and degree of moisture. Thus there is a need to study each site individually.

Heat exchange, or loss and gain, between indoors and outdoors is far less in below-ground structures than in above-ground ones. Yet there are temperature and humidity differences between below-ground and above-ground structures. In general, the below-ground space has higher relative humidity and seasonally stable temperatures. Earth mass and rock transfer humidity by the capillary system, while above-ground relative humidity is mostly introduced by the air. On the other hand, an air ventilation system can change the degree of relative humidity in the below-ground structure.

Our research findings point out that the optimal use of below-ground space is in regions with stressful climate. We define a stressful climate as hot-dry, such as the Sahara Desert, or cold-dry, such as central Canada. A knowledge of this fact becomes essential for companies exploring for minerals in such regions with a need to accommodate their laborers, engineers, and other employees.

VENTILATION

Ventilation can be passive (natural) or active (mechanical). When both are present two other systems can be introduced as well. These are passive inlet combined with active outlet, or active inlet combined with passive outlet. In civil defense shelter design, the Chinese prefer passive ventilation and use the active ventilation as a back-up system.[1] Passive ventilation is more effecitve in hilly or mountainous regions than in a flat area occupied by many above-ground structures.

A difference in temperature between the indoor below-ground space and the outdoors is usual. In winter the indoor temperature is higher and in summer it is lower. This difference in temperature introduces differences in pressure, thereby causing air movement and passive (natural) air ventilation (fig. 71). It is therefore essential to carefully design the inlet-outlet locations, orientation, and volume to insure air flow.

BELOW-GROUND SHANGHAI

Shanghai is the largest city in China and has a population of over eleven million people. Like many other Chinese cities it has a pressing space shortage. Shanghai has become very active in using subsurface space. In the last ten years more than 2 million square meters of subsurface floor space have been constructed, primarily for nonresidential use. Some of those usages are food storage, warehouses, silos, garages, hospitals, markets, restaurants, theaters, hotels, entertainment centers, factories, workshops, subways, subaqueous tunnels, and others.[2] The water table in Shanghai is high. In general, the depth of an underground building is

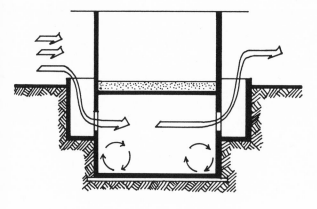

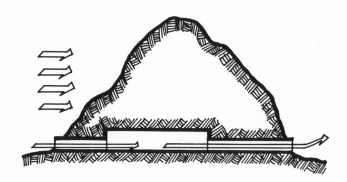

PASSIVE VENTILATION BY WIND PRESSURE

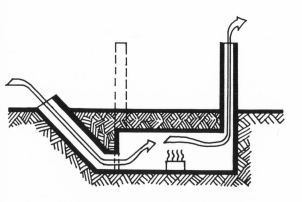

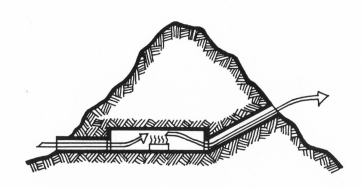

ACTIVE VENTILATION BY HEAT PRESSURE

Fig. 71. Passive and active ventilation systems in a below-ground space.

only 3 to 5 meters. The use of below-ground space in Shanghai is for the purpose of saving space in peacetime and for protection in wartime (including nuclear activities).

TONGJI UNIVERSITY RESEARCH

Shanghai Underground Research Group, located at Tongji University, is very active in underground space research. For the Third World, below-ground space is developed for utilities and transportation only. In developed countries it is used for the subway, shopping, theaters, and the like. Throughout China there are three stages in the development of underground space:

1. Transportation and storage: this stage started in Beijing and in Shanghai many years ago with a subway and tunnels built under rivers. Underground space includes pedestrian ways, water, sewage, and gas tunnels, and storage areas for grain. There are parking places for bicycles of working people and also some workshops and small factories.

2. Public buildings: department stores, hospitals, clubs, theaters, restaurants, hotels, and the like have been built underground. For example, Shanghai is involved with civil defense construction and is conducting research in this area. In China, Shanghai is in the second stage.

3. Future construction: a complex underground network of streets, subway lines and stops, along with commercial centers is planned. In Shanghai the subway is designed to have two intersecting lines (north-south and east-west) with a ring surrounding them. The north-south line is now under construction.

Shanghai faces many problems in the development of below-ground space. Its soil is soft. There are many problems associated with moisture, especially when there is no air conditioning. Another problem is the cost of building below ground due to the quality of the soil.

The Shanghai Underground Research Group's purpose is to keep people who stay below ground in good health and to design economical subterranean space that will compensate for the land price. The Research Group is divided into four teams: underground group for space use; underground engineering in soft ground; underground engineering in rocks; and a theoretical group with numerical calculation orientation.

The Research Group is presently designing food and grain storage facilities in Gong Xian, Henan Province, which is an improvement over the previous project that was built of bricks. This design of concrete, is under construction in the 1980s. The health issue is also of concern for people living and working below ground. Parameters in their research are primarily the ambient temperature and the relative humidity, yet they also deal with diversified issues such as oxygen, carbon dioxide, noise, light, color, architecture space, accessibility, ventilation, moisture, wind, volume, velocity, dust, odor, and radiation. This research team is composed of physicians, engineers, architects, health specialists, environmentalists, and members of other related fields. Current research projects in the 1980s are on hospitals and electrical equipment workshops.

THERMAL PERFORMANCE RESEARCH

This author's research in Shanghai was in col-

RESEARCHED SITES:

1. WORKERS' HOSPITAL
2. FURNITURE EXHIBITION HALL
3. DEPARTMENT STORE
4. WORKERS' CLUB
5. RESTAURANT

APPROXIMATE SCALE   0 1 2 3 4 5 KM

Fig. 72. The five sites researched in Shanghai.

laboration with the department of geotechnics of Tongji University. The research on thermal performance was conducted during the winter of 1984–85 and the summer of 1985. The prime goal of the research was to survey and evaluate the diurnal and the seasonal dry- and wet-bulb temperatures, as well as the relative humidity of a few selected nonresidential below-ground sites within Shanghai. For comparative analyses the temperature measurement was conducted on the hour diurnally and in two different seasons.

Five different sites in Shanghai were selected for our research (fig. 72). They differ in location, in design and, most important, in function. These sites were a workers' hospital; a furniture exhibition hall; a department store; a workers' club; and a restaurant. In each of the five case studies, temperature measurements were conducted in four indoor and outdoor sites of the structure for comparative analyses. Each underground structure was surveyed and mapped in detail in order to observe the relation between the design and the thermal performance of the building. We also conducted extensive interviews with the users and the managers of each of the five researched structures. Each of the buildings was photographed.

WORKERS' HOSPITAL

Located on a quiet street, the building is positioned diagonally to the street and is built more than eight floors above ground and one complete floor below ground. This below-ground floor is made of one structure more than 70 meters long and another small structure diagonal to it that is 13 meters long. The width of each structure is 12 meters. Most of the below-ground sections are taken up by three surgical operating rooms, and nearby are two large elevators, a stairway, a reception room, and a lengthy corridor (2 meters wide) along the linear structure in which there are a number of recuperation rooms on one side and small nurses' stations on the other. The recuperation rooms are without windows, being completely below-ground. They are occasionally ventilated by electrical means. Each of the recuperation rooms is divided into two parts, the small transitional space (5 by 2 meters) and the larger part (5 by 5 meters), which is the patients' room. Each of the patient wards has eight beds, four on each side. The design is simple and very practical. The space is lighted fluorescently.

The hospital was built between 1971 and 1976 and contains a total of 501 beds. The below-ground section has mechanical facilities for air intake, exhaust, dehumidification, water supply, and drainage. The below-ground section can accommodate 44 beds but was not occupied to capacity during our research visits (fig. 73). There was almost no postoperative infection from germs, as is also the case in the above-ground rooms (fig. 74). The patients stay underground for recovery (fig. 75). The dust is filtered out by the air-conditioning system.[3]

For comparison four sites were selected for dry- and wet-bulb temperature measurements, three of which are at the below-ground space (sites 1, 2, and 3) and the fourth (site 4) is at the outdoor site. The three below-ground sites are primarily the patients' rooms. Site 1 was not often used during our research while site 2 was more often inhabited by the patients. The patient rooms in the recovery area were used less than 50 percent during the time of our temperature measurements. These beds are below-ground, along with the operating rooms. The operating rooms are used for routine operations such as those on legs, arms, eyes, and stomachs, but not for heart operations. All the surgical patients stay below ground after the operations because, according to the doctors interviewed, flesh wounds heal faster in this environment and do not sweat. The doctors also estimate that the patients will recover in 10 to 30 percent less time than in above-ground space. On the other hand, the mending of bones does not occur any faster below ground. The air in the below-ground space is not considered fresh enough for heart operations, although the doctors admit that the stable temperature and humidity can contribute positively to such an operation.

The doctors pointed out the problems associated with this below-ground space, such as mosquitoes (in the winter due to the comfortable temperature), absence of natural light, and moisture. During the summer humidity may reach 80 percent or above and require the operation of a dehumidifier in order to bring the relative humidity to 60 percent. Since May and June are the rainy months in this area, a higher ratio of humidity occurs at that time. The doctors also indicated that active ventilation is noisy when operating and that the absence of windows eliminates any natural ventilation. Nevertheless the doctors interviewed prefer to work in the below-ground space because of its comfortable ambient temperature and humidity.

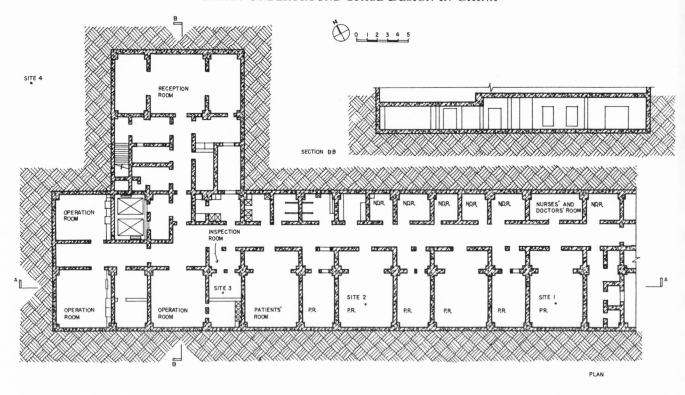

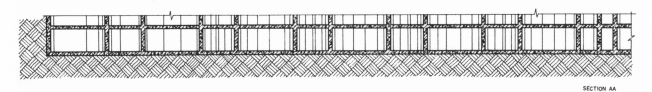

Fig. 73. Plan of the below-ground section of the Workers' Hospital, Shanghai. Note sites 1 to 4 selected for temperature measurements.

Thermal Performance. Although the operating and recreation rooms of the hospital are relatively shallow in depth (around 1 meter from ceiling to surface of the outdoor ground), the thermal performance of the underground sections is efficient. However, most of this below-ground space is covered by the tall (more than eight floors) above-ground structure of the rest of the hospital. The original motive for putting the operating and recreation rooms below-ground was for civil defense; only at a later time were the other advantages discovered in clinical performance.

Our major finding when interviewing the doctors was that patient recovery within the below-ground space saved 10 to 30 percent of the time required for recovery above ground. The major causes for this are the diurnal stability of temperature and relative humidity and the synchronization of the two. This stability provides

steady yet continuous ambient conditions for the healing of wounds. This finding certainly has economic implications in the saving of time, services, and space for patients, doctors, and administrative staff.

The temperature was measured in four sites, three of which were indoors (sites 1, 2, and 3) and one outdoors (site 4). The temperature was also measured by dry- and wet-bulb thermometers during a twenty-four hour period in summer (1–2 August 1985) and winter (22–23 December 1984).

Summer temperature (fig. 76) differs greatly between indoor and outdoor readings. Rooms 1, 2, and 3 show diurnally stable dry-bulb temperatures of 26 degrees C (79 degrees F) and similar stability in the wet-bulb temperature in sites 1 and 2 with readings of 23 degrees C (73.5 degrees F). The wet-bulb temperature is usually

Fig. 74. View of the corridor in the below-ground Workers' Hospital in Shanghai.

Fig. 75. One of the rooms researched in the below-ground Workers' Hospital in Shanghai.

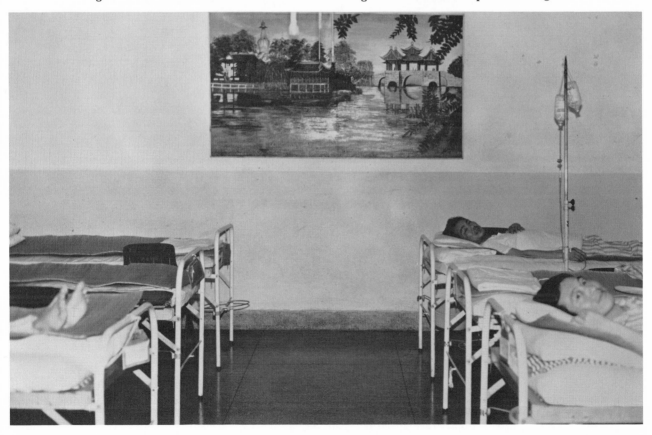

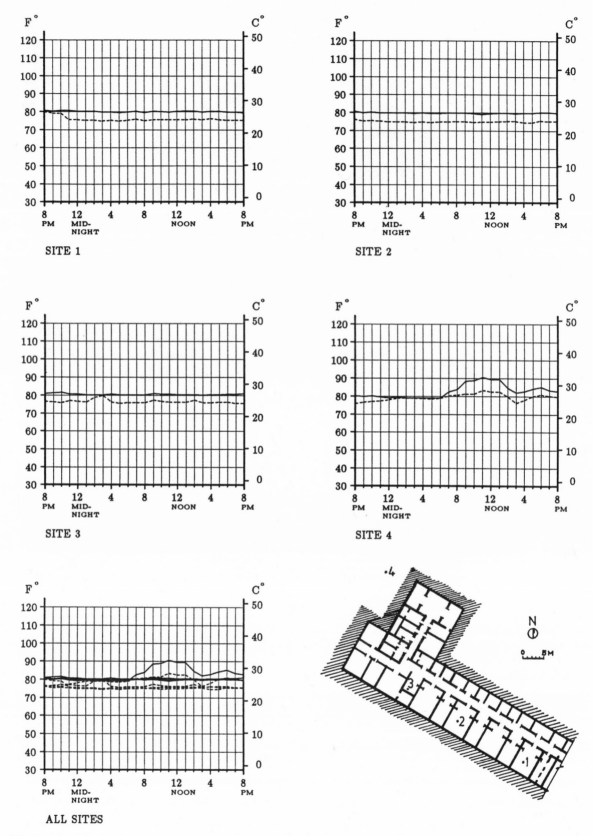

Fig. 76. Summer dry-bulb (solid line) and wet-bulb (broken line) temperatures of the underground hospital in Shanghai, measured on 1–2 August 1985.

lower than the dry-bulb temperature. Site 3 has some fluctuation in its wet-bulb temperature.

The outdoor temperature of the summer was in full contrast with the indoor temperature. Fluctuation occurred in both dry-bulb and wet-bulb temperatures, especially during the daytime, and became stable at night (dry-bulb) or almost stable (wet-bulb). However, the range between day and night dry-bulb outdoor temperatures was 32.5 degrees C (90.5 degrees F) (highest) and 26.4 degrees C (79.5 degrees F) (lowest). Similar but not identical was the wet-bulb temperature. In comparing all sites we found that the range of temperatures between maximum and minimum (both wet and dry) was small. An exception to this condition was the outdoor daytime temperature.

The winter temperatures (fig. 77) of the indoor rooms were quite different from each other. The most diurnally stable among the three was site 3, which was a small, compact room. There was, however, frequent fluctuation in sites 1 and 2. We think that this fluctuation was caused by interference of outside air currents through the corridor. In either case, the rooms required a little heat in order to bring them to a comfortable ambient temperature. The outdoor temperature, however, was less than 0 degrees C (32 degrees F) during the twenty-four hours.

Summer relative humidity is very high and all four sites measured in the hospital were above 80 percent for most of the twenty-four hours (fig. 78). In site 1 summer relative humidity was stable at around 83 percent during the twenty-four hours except in the evening, when it reached almost 100 percent. The other underground recovery room (site 2) also had stable humidity (around 82) percent during the twenty-four hours with little, if any, fluctuation. At site 3 relative humidity fluctuated during the twenty-four hours, even sometimes reaching almost 100 percent at 3:00 a.m. and going down to 80 percent in the evening.

Winter relative humidity is usually much lower and fluctuates more than that of the summer. The indoor winter relative humidity of site 1 has an exceptional increase, reaching almost 100 percent late at night and then dropping sharply to around 75 percent before noon. In the other below-ground room (site 2), relative humidity fluctuated diurnally and went down from around 80 percent in the evening to around 50 percent before noon. A similar development pattern takes place in the third indoor room (site 3).

The relative humidity that fluctuated most was at the outdoor site (site 4), in which an extreme fluctuation occurred almost every hour. Indeed, it seemed to us that this extreme outdoor fluctuation influenced the indoor fluctuation to a limited extent. It is worth mentioning here that a Shanghai winter lacks rain and what little precipitation there is is in the form of snow. Yet Shanghai itself is located adjacent to a huge body of water.

Graphs of the three indoor sites show the total range of fluctuation to be between 50 to 100 percent for relative humidity in the winter, while the summer fluctuation shows a range of between 80 to 100 percent. Evidently, the steady relative humdity of the summer does speed recovery and healing more than in the winter, when the humidity is relatively less steady.

In conclusion, the temperature stability of sites 1 and 2, especially in the summer, contributes to the comfort of the patients. Consequently wounds heal in a shorter time than above ground. We surmise also that the stability of the humidity in sites 1 and 2 reinforces these results.

Both summer and winter below-ground ambient temperatures are relatively tolerable and comfortable. In the winter, a little heat may be required to make the rooms more comfortable. Indoor summer conditions require a design that will bring about more air circulation and thus provide lower temperatures and less humidity.

We recommend the following design improvements:

1. All patients' rooms should be wider, have higher ceilings, and include an air shaft leading to the roof of the above-ground part of the hospital. The air shaft should have a wind catcher.
2. The corridor should be wider to facilitate passive air circulation and both ends should lead to the outside stairway opening.
3. Access to below-ground space should be as direct as possible to the main below-ground corridor. The connection should be made with a minimum of curves to enable the air to circulate to the two ends of the corridor.

FURNITURE EXHIBITION HALL

The below-ground Furniture Exhibition Hall was opened in March 1982 and has been used as such since then. The shortage of space above-ground led to the idea of using the below-ground space as an exhibition hall.

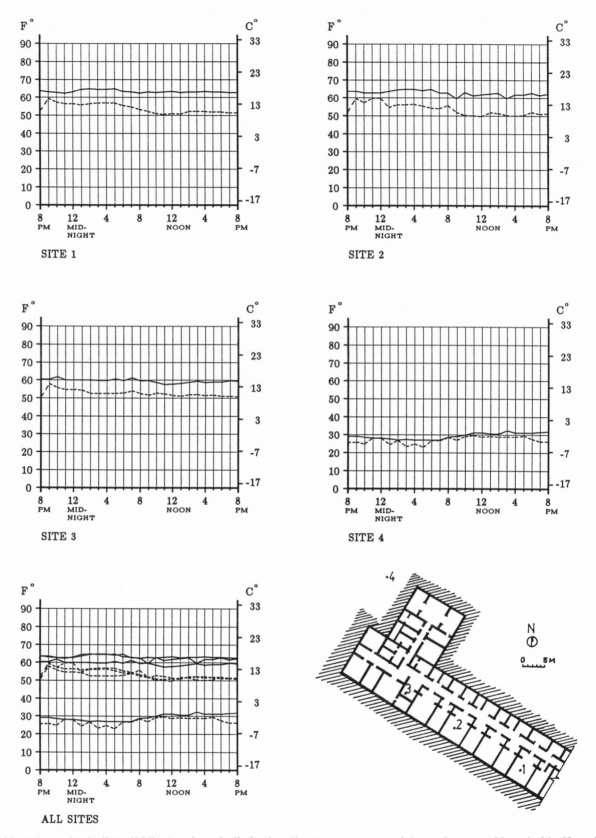

Fig. 77. Winter dry-bulb (solid line) and wet-bulb (broken line) temperatures of the underground hospital in Shanghai, measured on 22–23 December 1984.

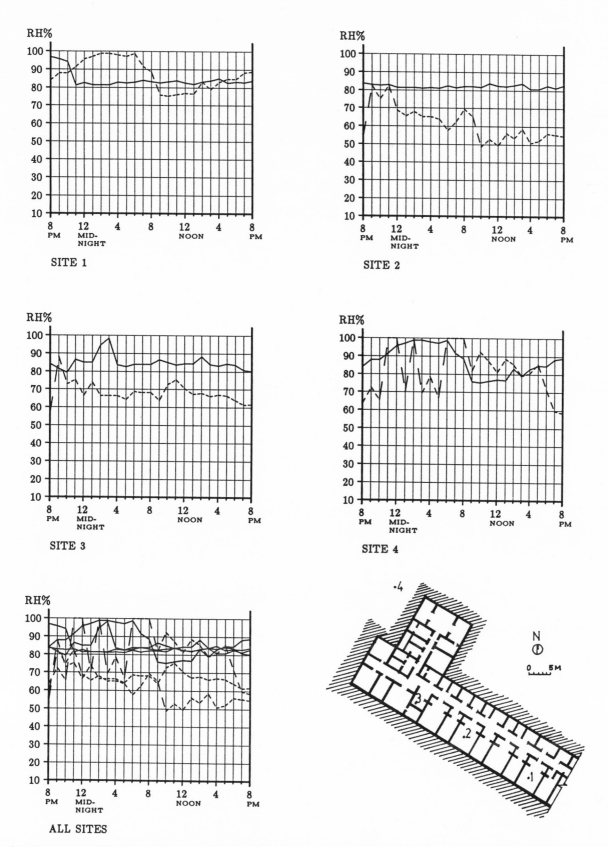

Fig. 78. Summer (solid line) and winter (broken line) relative humidity in the below-ground modern hospital, Shang-hai.

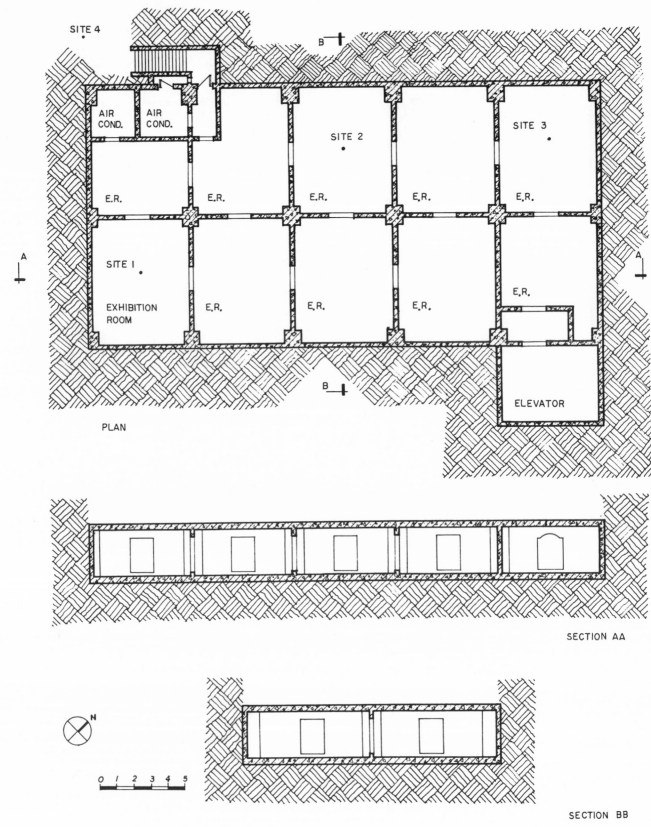

SITE 4

B

SITE 2

SITE 3

AIR
COND.

AIR
COND.

E.R.

E.R.

E.R.

E.R.

E.R.

A

A

SITE I

E.R.

E.R.

E.R.

E.R.

EXHIBITION
ROOM

E.R.

ELEVATOR

B

PLAN

SECTION AA

N

0 1 2 3 4 5

SECTION BB

Fig. 79. Plan and crosssection of the Furniture Exhibition Hall, Shanghai.

The part of the building below-ground is constructed of reinforced concrete with asphalt for waterproofing. The thickness of the ceiling is 1 meter. The hall consists of ten rooms of 43 square meters each (fig. 79). There is also another working space below ground. The entire five-story structure totals 2,150 square meters.

Advantages of the hall are primarily those of space and comfort. The stable temperature of the hall is suitable for furniture display during the winter and most of the summer (the hall has ventilation for air exchange during the morning in the summer). Thus temperature stability during the summer and winter occurs because of the diurnal and seasonal low amplitude. Above ground furniture is subject to contraction and expansion due to diurnal temperature changes.

The biggest problem encountered in the Furniture Exhibition Hall is high humidity. During the rainy summer season in the months of June, July, and August, the hall must use a dehumidifier six hours a day, especially during June. In winter the humidity in the hall is 50 percent and may reach 80 percent during the summer. Because of the humidity the exhibition hall needs to change furniture every few months.

Thermal Performance. The Furniture Exhibition Hall displays newly built and custom-made furniture (fig. 80). The owners wish to keep the furniture in a stable environment so that it can retain its quality throughout the season. The space is used for exhibiting furniture in addition to storing it. Here too, we measured the dry-bulb and wet-bulb temperatures in both summer and winter in three indoor sites (sites 1, 2, and 3) and one outdoor site (site 4).

Summer temperatures show a contrast between the indoor and the outdoor sites (fig. 81). The indoor sites are in general more stable than the outdoor site diurnally. Site 1 dry-bulb temperatures range between 27.6 degrees C (81.5 degrees F) after midnight and 29.2 degrees C

Fig. 80. View of rooms in the Furniture Exhibition Hall.

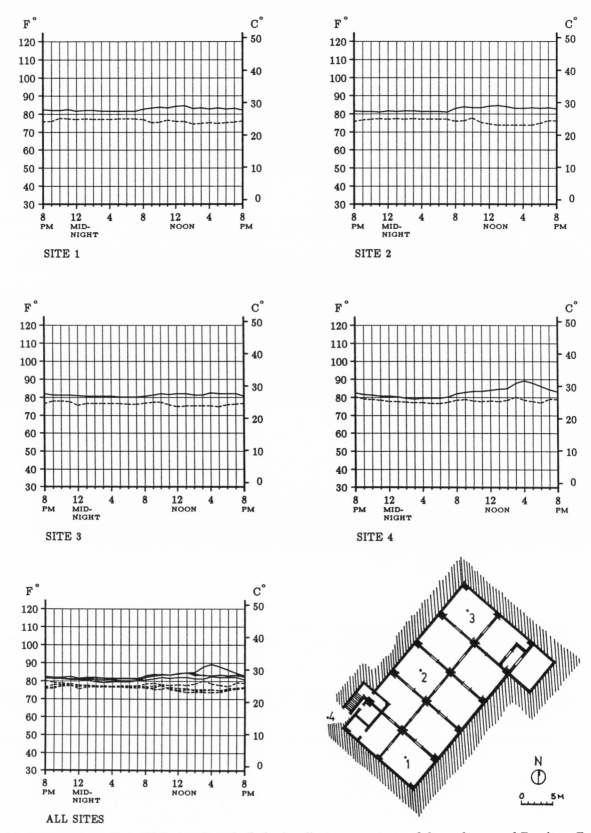

Fig. 81. Summer dry-bulb (solid line) and wet-bulb (broken line) temperatures of the underground Furniture Exhibition Hall, measured on 2–3 August 1985. All sites are below-ground except site 3, which is located at the street level.

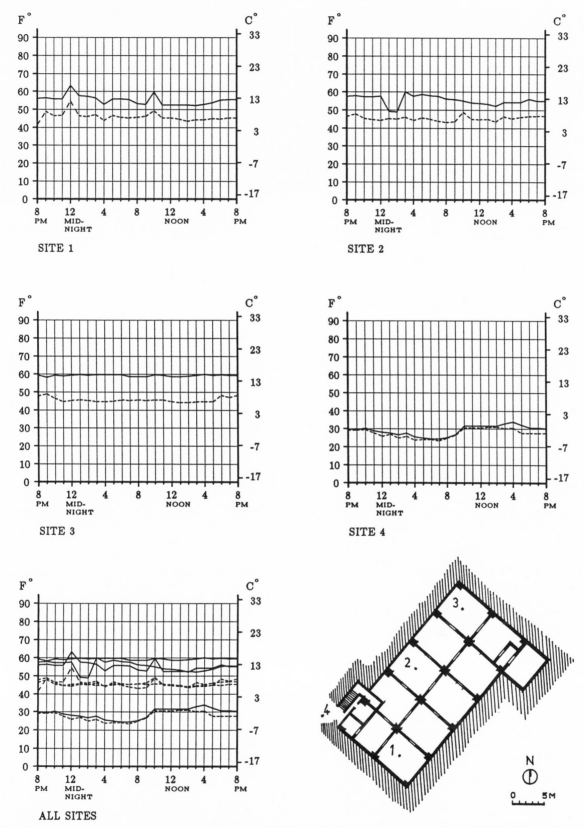

SITE 1

SITE 2

SITE 3

SITE 4

ALL SITES

Fig. 82. Winter dry-bulb (solid line) and wet-bulb (broken line) temperatures of the underground Furniture Exhibition Hall, measured 23–24 December 1984.

(84.5 degrees F) at 1:00 P.M., which still falls near the comfort zone. Site 2 follows almost the same pattern as in site 1 in both dry- and wet-bulb temperatures. In both cases the little instability takes place during the day while it is more stable during the night. A similar condition exists in site 3 as well. It should be noted that all the rooms of the below-ground Furniture Exhibition Hall are connected to each other with open doorways that serve to balance the temperature in all rooms. The outdoor temperature at site 4 fluctuates more. The peak of the dry-bulb temperature is at 4:00 P.M. (31.8 degrees C or 89 degrees F) and its lowest point is at 5:00 A.M. (26.2 degrees C or 79 degrees F). In any case, the stability of the temperature maintained the quality of the wood.

The winter temperatures of the underground Furniture Exhibition Hall fluctuate more than those of the summer (fig. 82). We believe this is due to the intrusion of the outdoor temperature into the indoor space. The building has a huge elevator that brings in with it some cold outside air when in use. Site 1 has a temperature range between 11.2 degrees C (52 degrees F) at 3:00 P.M. and 17.4 degrees C (63 degrees F) at midnight. Site 2 dry-bulb temperature fluctuates primarily after midnight and in the afternoon. The maximum dry-bulb temperature is 14.4 degrees C (58 degrees F) at 9:00 P.M. and the lowest is 9.4 degrees C (49 degrees F) at 2:00 A.M. Site 3, located in a corner room of the below-ground Furniture Exhibition Hall and therefore a site with outdoor air intrusion, introduces a stable dry- and wet-bulb temperature. Its dry-bulb temperature ranges between 14.6 degrees C (58 degrees F) at 9:00 P.M. to 15.4 degrees C (59.5 degrees F) after midnight. The outdoors (site 4) is certainly distinctly different from the three indoor sites since all its temperatures were below zero degrees C except for the hour of 4:00 P.M. The temperature fluctuation pattern of site 4 is entirely different from the fluctuation patterns of sites 1 and 2, which leads us to believe that there was an outdoor air intrusion at sites 1 and 2.

Summer relative humidity of the below-ground Furniture Exhibition Hall ranges between 65 and 85 percent at the indoor sites and between 65 and 93 percent at the outdoor site (fig. 83). In the indoor site 1, relative humidity ranges between 70 and 84 percent, being stable almost all night and still relatively stable throughout the day. This range is acceptable for

the preservation of furniture. The important position of site 1 helps its relative stability since it is out of the line of possible outdoor air intrusion during the use of the elevator. Site 2 has a similar general pattern since it is relatively stable at night (when the elevator is not in use) and less stable during the daytime. The differentiation between the highest relative humidity at night (around 85 percent) and the lowest in the daytime (around 64 percent) is still acceptable for the maintenance of the furniture. Site 3, which is also located in a corner, has a pattern similar to that of site 1 and has relatively more diurnal stability than site 2. The range between night and day is also relatively smaller than in sites 1 and 2. Here too, most of the night relative humidity is stable although the daytime relative humidity fluctuates somewhat. The outdoor relative humidity of the summer in site 4 fluctuates greatly in the day but is much more stable during the night at around 90 percent.

The winter relative humidity in all the indoor sites is lower than that of the summer and fluctuated much more (fig. 83). The outdoor relative humidity (site 4) also fluctuates diurnally, yet it is sometimes higher than that of the summer. The relative humidity of site 1 fluctuates between a low of 50 percent after midnight to a high of 68 percent before noon. Site 2's relative humidity ranges between 37 percent at midnight to 70 percent before noon. Site 3 has the lowest relative humidity of the indoor sites, ranging between 37 percent and 58 percent. As in the other cases, the outdoor relative humidity (site 4) is much different from the indoor ones. Here the relative humidity reached 100 percent in the evening and again in the morning and went down to 68 percent in the late afternoon, with much diurnal fluctuation. Much of the time the relative humidity of the winter is higher than that of the summer.

DEPARTMENT STORE

Department Store No. 9 consists of both above- and below-ground space. The below-ground part consists of a large number of small rooms used for storage and shopping (fig. 84). According to the workers at the department store, the building is comfortable except in the summer, when they have high humidity due to the rain. Some products can be stored here that can withstand the summer humidity. The winter is warm and comfortable.

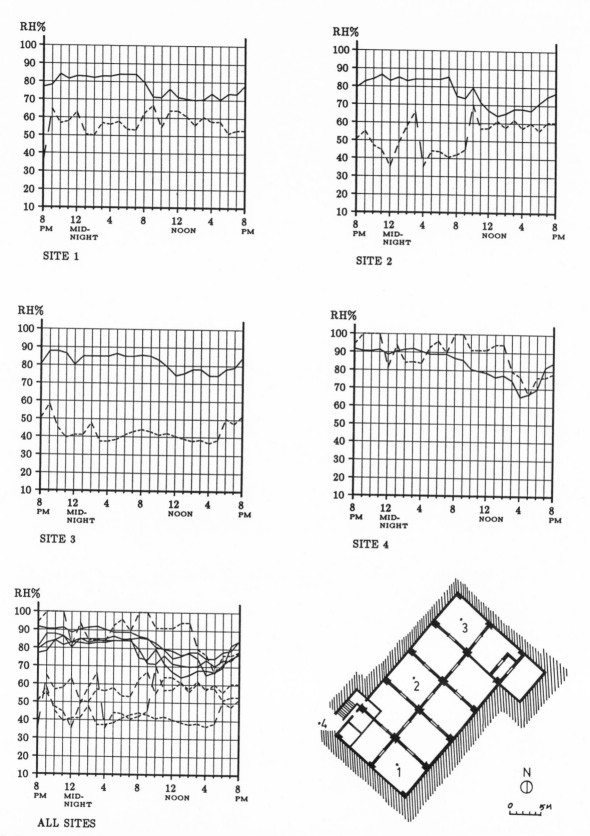

Fig. 83. Summer (solid line) and winter (broken line) relative humidity in the below-ground Furniture Exhibition Hall.

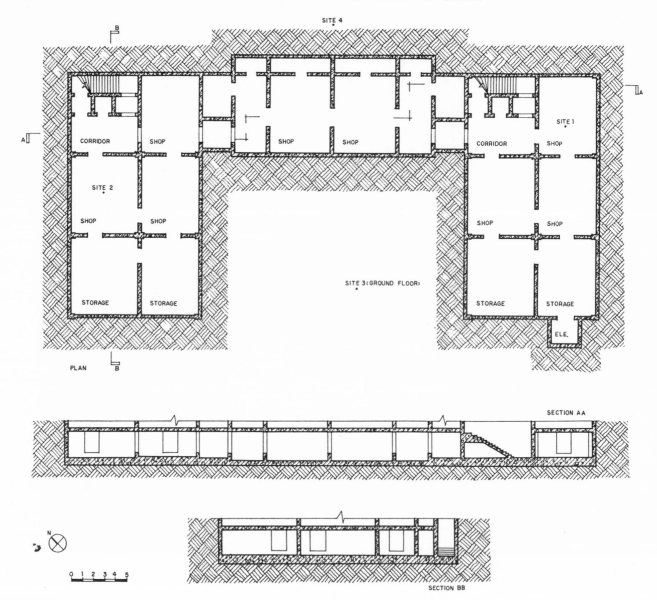

Fig. 84. Plan and crosssection of Department Store No. 9 in Shanghai. Note sites for temperature measurements. Site 3 is on the street level.

The problems associated with the below-ground section of the building are ventilation and high summer humidity. Ventilation is limited (the air inlet is too small) and there is a need for air exchange. According to the users there is less oxygen in the air there than in places above ground. Sometimes when the space is crowded with people employees and customers experience headaches or dizziness. During the rainy months of the summer season the humidity is high and a dehumidifier is needed. A water cooling tower was built in 1981.

Thermal Performance. Below-ground Department Store No. 9 is located on one of the most crowded streets of Shanghai. It is a medium-sized store occupying the ground floor and one floor below ground. Both are used for display and sales as well as for storage. Four sites were measured, two of which were located on the below-ground floor, one on the ground floor, and the other outdoors in the street near the department store. The ground floor site, located in the middle of the hall facing the large entrance to the department store, was therefore influenced

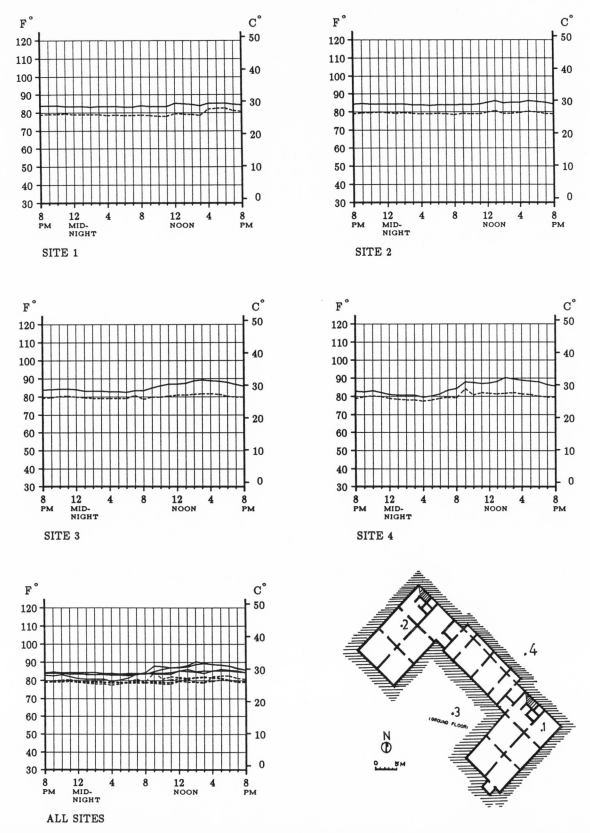

Fig. 85. Summer dry-bulb (solid line) and wet-bulb (broken line) temperatures of the below-ground Department Store No. 9, measured on 4–5 August 1985. Site 3 is on the street level floor and site 4 is outdoors.

by the intrusion of outdoor temperatures. In addition the department store was very crowded with shoppers during some hours of the day, which also influenced the diurnal temperatures.

Summer temperatures of the below-ground sites (sites 1 and 2) are stable and almost identical in both the dry- and wet-bulb temperatures (fig. 85). Site 1 has a temperature range from 28.4 degrees C (83 degrees F) in the morning to 29.6 degrees C (85 degrees F) early in the evening, dry-bulb temperature. Similarly, site 2 has a dry-bulb temperature of 28.7 degrees C (83.5 degrees F) at 5:00 A.M. to 30 degrees C (86 degrees F) at 5:00 P.M. In both sites this is a reasonable and comfortable ambient temperature. Yet both sites suffer from lack of ventilation. Site 3 has a fluctuation of dry-bulb temperature, being high in the afternoon because of the intensity of shoppers visiting the department store and lower at night when the store is closed. Its dry-bulb temperature ranges from the lowest of 28.1 degrees C (82.5 degrees F) at 6:00 A.M. to 31.8 degrees C (89 degrees F) at 3:00 P.M. Site 4, the outdoor location, fluctuated the most during the twenty-four hours. Its highest dry-bulb temperature was 32.4 degrees C (90 degrees F) at 2:00 P.M. and its lowest was 26.4 degrees C (79.5 degrees F) at 4:00 A.M.

The wet-bulb temperature is almost parallel to the dry-bulb temperature diurnally in both fluctuation and steadiness. Usually the difference between wet-bulb and dry-bulb temperatures is around three degrees C in sites 1 and 2, and two to five degrees C in sites 3 and 4. As usual, the wet-bulb temperatures are lower than the dry-bulb temperatures.

Winter dry-bulb temperatures of the below-ground sites are similar in sites 1 and 2 while the site 3 temperature and that of the outdoors (site 4) follow a different pattern (fig. 86). Sites 1 and 2 are more stable although they fluctuate in the afternoon and before midnight. The dry-bulb and wet-bulb temperatures parallel each other, with a differentiation of around 5 degrees C. Both temperatures are relatively comfortable, yet a little heating was needed to make the sites more comfortable. The dry-bulb temperature of site 1 ranges from a low of 12 degrees C (54 degrees F) at noon to 14.2 degrees C (57.5 degrees F) at 1:00 P.M. Similarly, in Site 2 dry-bulb temperatures range from a low of 10.6 degrees C (51 degrees F) toward the end of the night to a high of 12.8 degrees C (55 degrees F) at 4:00 P.M. Site 3 fluctuation occurred primarily in the

afternoon while it was stable at night in both dry- and wet-bulb temperatures. Its maximum dry-bulb temperature occurred at 3:00 P.M. at 9.2 degrees C (48.5 degrees F), the minimum dry-bulb temperature of 4.6 degrees C (40 degrees F) occurred at 8:00 A.M. The outdoor temperatures in site 4 fluctuated greatly during the tested twenty-four-hour period. Its dry-bulb temperature dropped to -1.2 degrees C (30 degrees F) at 6:00 A.M. and rose to a maximum of 4.2 degrees C (39.5 degrees F) at 1:00 P.M. Wet-bulb temperatures of site 4 are almost identical to the dry-bulb temperatures at night, while during the daytime they are lower by a range of 2 to 3 degrees C.

Relative humidity in the below-ground department store is shown in figure 87. Summer indoor relative humidity shows much more diurnal stability than that of the winter. The range between summer and winter is relatively great in the below-ground space (sites 1 and 2) and becomes smaller at the above-ground space (site 3) and the outdoor site (site 4).

Summer relative humidity of site 1 is reasonably stable during most of the time (around 82 percent) and with an increase to 90 percent in the evening only. The changes in the evening, however, can be attributed to the flow of customers since this is a closed room without windows or ventilation. The other room (site 2) has much more stable relative humidity (around 82 percent diurnally). The indoor above-ground (site 3) has a diurnally fluctuating relative humidity between 90 percent at 7:00 A.M. and 75 percent during the afternoon. Yet the nighttime relative humidity steadily increases with little fluctuation compared to that of the daytime. The outdoor summer relative humidity (site 4) is quite high (around 90 percent) during the entire night with a drop to around 72 percent in the afternoon, with much fluctuation during the day.

Winter relative humidity is quite different in pattern and range from that of the summer, diurnally. In site 1, except at 9:00 A.M., when relative humidity reaches almost 80 percent, the range of relative humidity throughout the day is between a low of 58 percent at the end of the night to a high of 70 percent in the afternoon. Yet there is more stability during the night than in the day. The relative humidity of site 2 also ranges between a low of 50 percent at 11:00 P.M. to an exceptionally high relative humidity of 70 percent at noon. The relative humidity fluctuates diurnally, yet it is much lower than that of the

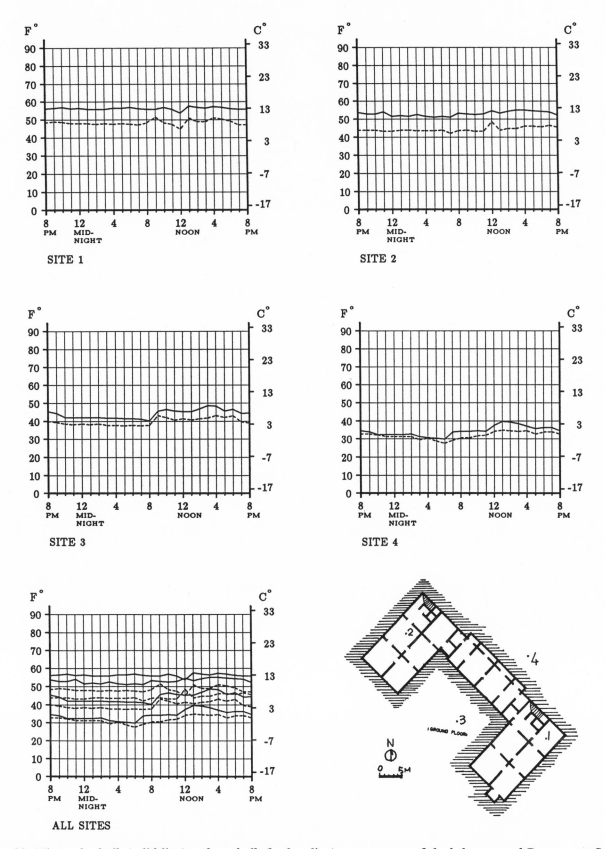

Fig. 86. Winter dry-bulb (solid line) and wet-bulb (broken line) temperatures of the below-ground Department Store No. 9, measured on 4–5 August 1985. Site 3 is on the street level floor and site 4 is outdoors.

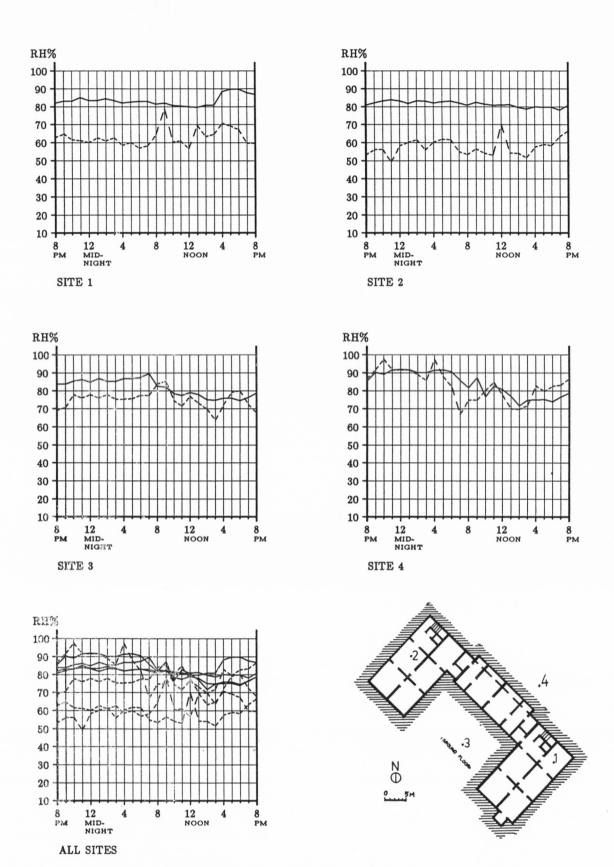

Fig. 87. Summer (solid line) and winter (broken line) relative humidity of the below-ground department store, Shanghai.

summertime throughout the twenty-four hours. The above-ground indoor site 3 has a higher winter relative humidity than the other two indoor sites, ranging from between 85 percent at 9:00 A.M. to a low of 65 percent at 3:00 P.M. Here again much diurnal fluctuation takes place and in some hours (between 8–9:00 A.M. and 3–4:00 P.M.) the relative humidity of the winter is higher than that of the summer. This is due to the intrusion of outdoor relative humidity into the department store through the large main door in the front of the store. The outdoor diurnal relative humidity (site 4) has a large range of differentiation, as high as 98 percent at 10:00 P.M. and 4:00 A.M. and as low as 67 percent at 7:00 A.M. In some hours of the night and the daytime the winter relative humidity exceeds that of the summer, although it is lower most of the time.

WORKERS' CLUB

The building that houses the Workers' Club was constructed in 1979. The goal was to build a civil defense shelter and use it as a club as well. The total floor area below-ground is around 1,000 square meters (fig. 88). The soil above the club is used as a garden and is surrounded by buildings not used for defense. According to the local manager this area is good for recreation so it was worth constructing the building.

The space below ground is used for large meetings in which as many as three hundred people at one time might be seated. In the afternoon it is used for television (250 persons) or performances on a smaller scale. There is dancing in the evenings. This space is normally used every day both in the summer and winter (fig. 89), although more people use the Worker's Club in the winter than during the summer. In the summer there is air conditioning and an active ventilation system in use during large gatherings. In the winter no heaters are used but ventilation is utilized. Also dehumidifiers are used in the summer and sometimes in the winter. The ventilation, air conditioning, and dehumidification were planned and constructed with the building. Sewage must be pumped because of the low elevation.

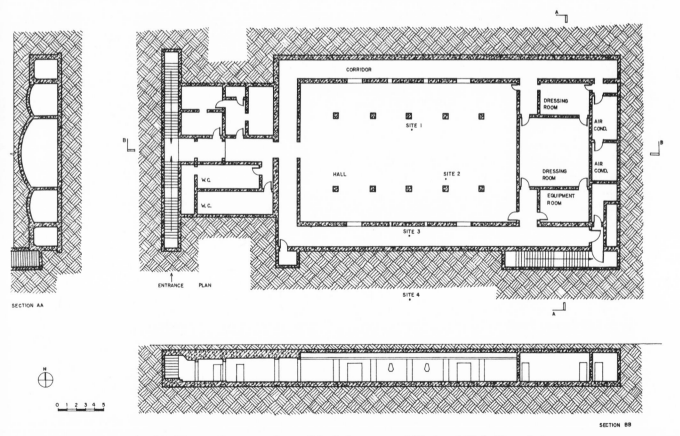

Fig. 88. Plan and crosssections of the below-ground Workers' Club, Shanghai.

Fig. 89. View inside the Workers' Club researched in Shanghai.

According to the manager of the Worker's Club, the main problem is the limited air exchange, especially when there is a gathering of more than one hundred people in the club. Other problems associated with the building are that it is too warm in the summer when dancing takes place and that there is too much humidity in the air in the summer, which requires the use of a dehumidifier. Some equipment is damaged by the high humidity. The manager suggests the need for the improvement of the ventilation system and the introduction of more air circulation. *Thermal Performance.* The below-ground Workers' Club is composed of primarily large halls used for meetings, social gatherings, and so on. When we monitored the temperature there in the summer crowds of young people were dancing, mostly between 7:00 and 11:00 P.M. At 9:00 P.M., 230 people were in the hall on the first evening. On the second day the hall was again crowded, with around 250 people at 2:00 P.M.;

one-half of that number during the afternoon, and approximately 250 people again at 8:00 P.M.

Indoor summer temperatures (dry-bulb and wet-bulb) are presented in sites 1, 2, and 3 (fig. 90). Site 4 represents the outdoor temperature. Sites 1 and 2, which show temperatures within the halls at two different places, are almost identical. The increase in dry-bulb and wet-bulb temperatures in sites 1 and 2 takes place in the evening until 10:00 P.M., then drops and becomes almost steady until the next day at 1:00 P.M., when it rises again. This increase of temperature obviously occurs because of the large number of people present in the hall. The dry- and wet-bulb temperatures also parallel each other in both sites with a difference of two degrees C or less. The range of dry-bulb temperatures for site 1 is between 27.8 degrees C (82 degrees F), which is the lowest at the second part of the night, and 30.2 degrees C (86.5 degrees F) at 3:00 P.M. Site 2 has a low dry-bulb tem-

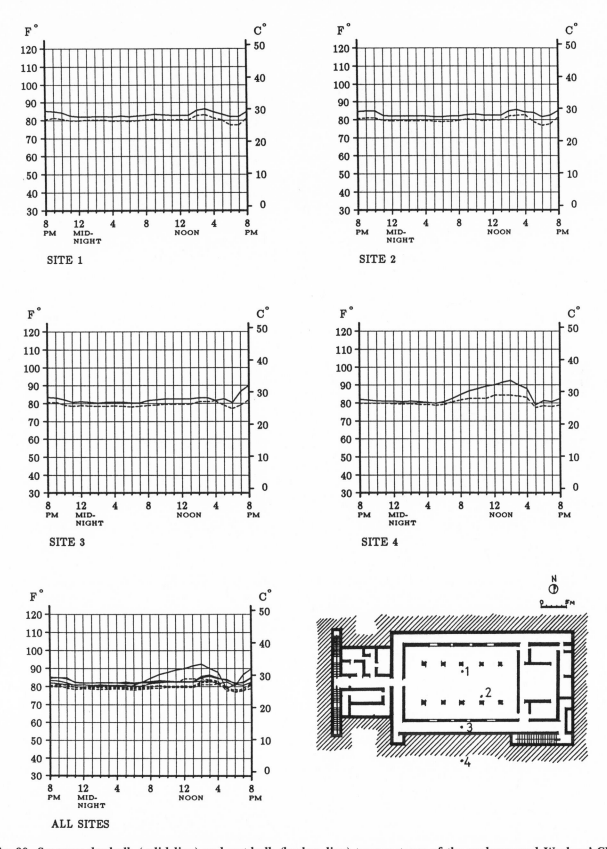

SITE 1

SITE 2

SITE 3

SITE 4

ALL SITES

Fig. 90. Summer dry-bulb (solid line) and wet-bulb (broken line) temperatures of the underground Workers' Club, measured on 3–4 August 1985.

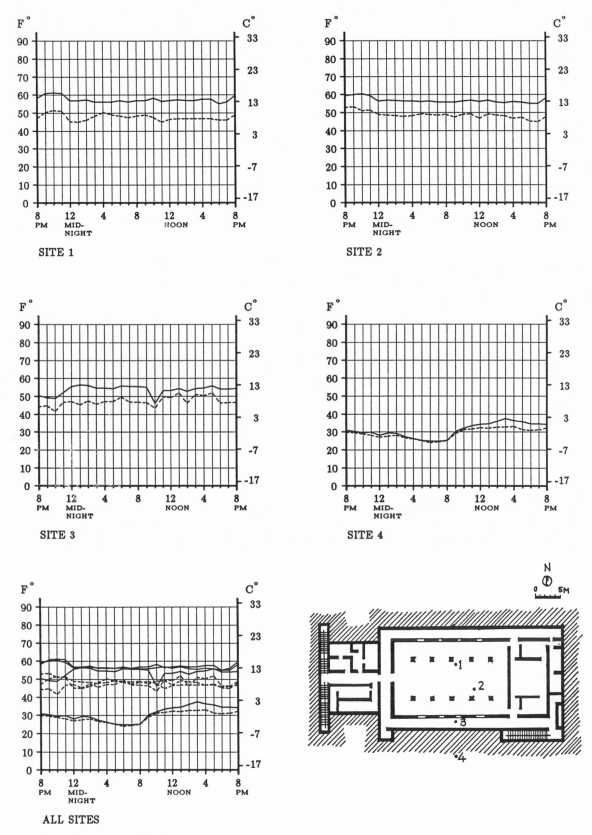

Fig. 91. Winter dry-bulb (solid line) and wet-bulb (broken line) temperatures of the underground Workers' Club, measured 24–25 December 1984.

perature of 27.6 degrees C (81.5 degrees F) at the end of the night and 29.8 degrees C (85.5 degrees F) at 3:00 P.M. Site 3, which is used as a corridor, shows a slight difference in pattern from sites 1 and 2. Its lowest dry-bulb temperature takes place at the end of the night with 26.8 degrees C (80 degrees F) and its highest temperature occurs at 8:00 P.M. with 32.2 degrees C (90 degrees F). Site 3 has wet-bulb temperatures that are similar to the dry-bulb and usually are lower by one to two degrees. Site 4, the outdoor temperature, has its highest peak in the afternoon with 33.6 degrees C (92.5 degrees F) dry-bulb temperature at 2:00 P.M. and 26.6 degrees C (80 degrees F) at its lowest point at 5:00 A.M. The wet-bulb temperatures for site 4 also fluctuates but less than those of the dry-bulb temperatures.

Winter temperature is presented in figure 91. Here too the hall was occupied by more than two hundred people from 8:00 to 11:00 P.M. on the first evening. Also there was a reasonable number of people in the hall during the other hours. Sites 1 and 2, which are located in the large hall, are similar to each other but not identical. In Site 1 the wet-bulb temperature is almost parallel to the dry-bulb temperature. There is a range of difference of 4 to 7 degrees C between them. The dry-bulb temperature, however, fluctuates primarily between 8:00 and 11:00 P.M. and between 5:00 and 8:00 P.M. It is almost stable during the other hours of the day. The lowest dry-bulb temperature is 13.4 degrees C (56 degrees F) at the end of the evening and the highest is 16.2 degrees C (61 degrees F) at 10:00 P.M. Obviously the rise in temperature in the evening results from the larger crowd accommodated in the hall. Site 2 is much like site 1 in its fluctuation pattern and temperature differences occur mostly with the wet-bulb temperature. Site 4 dry-bulb temperatures range from the highest of 3.0 degrees C (37.5 degrees F) at 3:00 P.M. to the lowest of -4 degrees C (24.5 degrees F) at 6:00 A.M. Both dry- and wet-bulb temperatures of the site occasionally parallel each other. Nevertheless both temperatures of site 4 are way below the average of the other three sites.

Relative humidity of the below-ground Workers' Club indicates relative stability in the summer and less stability in the winter, with a large range between winter and summer at the indoor sites (fig. 92). Summer relative humidity of site 1 has a small diurnal range between a high of 93 percent at 1:00 A.M. to a low of 83 percent be-

tween 6:00 and 7:00 P.M. Site 2 has a similar pattern of stability for most of the twenty-four hours: it hovers around 90 percent relative humidity, with highest, 94 percent, occurring at 4:00 P.M., and the lowest, 82 percent, at 5:00 P.M. Similar patterns took place in site 3 (corridor), where the summer relative humidity is almost stable, averaging around 91 percent most of the time with the exception of 98 percent at 4:00 P.M. and a drop to 74 percent at 7:00 P.M. The outdoor (site 4) summer relative humidity is exceptional and ranges from around 95 percent throughout the night, with a fluctuated drop during the day to a low of 74 percent.

The winter relative humidity pattern (fig. 92) differs from the summer one, introducing much lower humidity and larger diurnal fluctuations at the indoor sites. Most of the time the winter relative humidity in the three indoor sites is much lower than that of the summer relative humidity. At site 1, winter relative humidity ranges between the extreme of 72 percent at 4:00 A.M. to a low of 43 percent at 11:00 A.M., with much diurnal fluctuation. In indoor site 2 the relative humidity fluctuates less and ranges between a high of 70 percent at 8:00 P.M. to a low of 53 percent at 7:00 P.M. In the aboveground indoor site 3, relative humidity fluctuates diurnally between a low of 50 percent at 1:00 A.M. to a high of 88 percent at 1:00 P.M., with frequent fluctuation because of the immediate outdoor influence. The outdoor relative humidity of site 4 is exceptionally high, especially in the morning between 4:00 and 8:00 A.M., when it reaches 100 percent and then drops sharply to 69 percent at 3:00 P.M. Most of the time this winter relative humidity is higher than that of the summertime.

RESTAURANT

The restaurant monitored in our research is also located in Shanghai. The below-ground space has been used as a restaurant since the end of 1979 and consists of five major dining rooms plus other below-ground dining space (fig. 93). The kitchen is upstairs. Each dining room has five to six four-person tables. The restaurant can accommodate two hundred or more people in the below-ground space for lunch or dinner or the space can be rented for special parties. The restaurant is especially crowded on Saturday and Sunday with young people who smoke and come for drinks and dinner. Customers find the

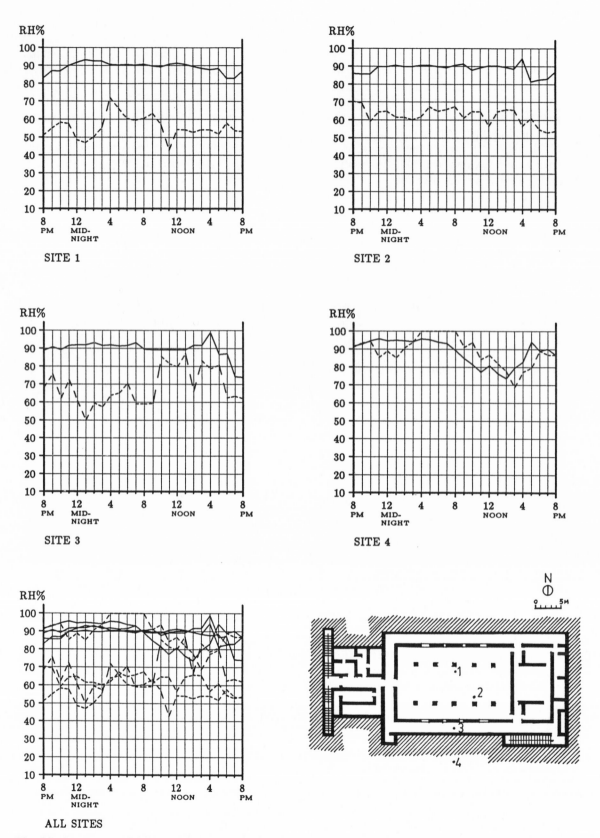

Fig. 92. Summer (solid line) and winter (broken line) relative humidity of the below-ground Workers' Club.

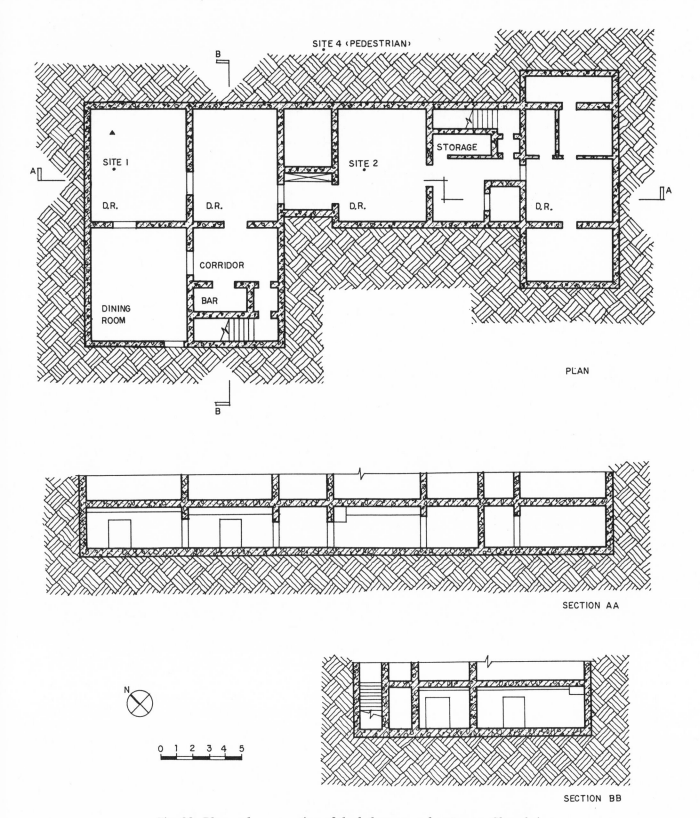

SITE 4 ‹PEDESTRIAN›

B

SITE 1

▲

D.R.

D.R.

A

A

SITE 2

STORAGE

D.R.

D.R.

CORRIDOR

BAR

DINING
ROOM

B

B

PLAN

SECTION AA

N

0 1 2 3 4 5

SECTION BB

Fig. 93. Plan and crosssection of the below-ground restauran, Shanghai.

rooms intimate and suited to their needs. It is a relatively quiet place except for sounds from other customers.

Problems associated with the restaurant are shortage of ventilation, pollution, and the low ceiling of the below-ground sections. Since the space must be ventilated during the summer and the winter, the ventilation system should be enlarged. Smoking by the customers increases pollution and instigates customer complaints. The ceiling in the below-ground section of the restaurant is only 2.5 meters high and is way below the height considered average in buildings used for public gatherings. Since heat rises, the occupants of the restaurant experience discomfort in the low-ceilinged section especially when cigarette smoking is permitted. The positioning of the walls to create rooms limits air movement and creates "air pockets." Mobile low walls would permit more ventilation yet still give the intimate atmosphere desired by customers. Also there is only one entrance to the restaurant which represents a fire hazard.

Thermal Performance. This is a medium-sized restaurant that consists of the ground floor and one below-ground floor. We studied four sites, three of them indoors. Of these two are located below-ground (sites 1 and 2) and one is on the ground floor (site 3). Site 4 is located outdoors in the street.

Summer temperatures of sites 1 and 2 are very similar to each other (fig. 94). Both locations are almost a closed environment, having no windows or kitchens. In both sites the dry- and wet-bulb temperatures are steady and parallel each other between 8:00 P.M. and 10:00 A.M. During this period the dry-bulb temperature is between 28.4 degrees C (83 degrees F) and 27.8 degrees C (82 degrees F). The fluctuation begins at noon and continues until the evening. Evidentlly the customers' presence influences those changes during the afternoon hours. In site 1 the dry-bulb afternoon temperature changes from 25.6 degrees C (78 degrees F) at noon to 29 degrees C (84.5 degrees F) at 3:00 P.M., then drops to 25.8 degrees C (78.5 degrees F) at 5:00 P.M. Site 3 shows less fluctuation during the twenty-four hours and its dry-bulb temperature range goes from the low point of 26.2 degrees C (79 degrees F) in the early morning to the high point of 28.9 degrees C (84 degrees F) at 8:00 P.M. However, on the day we measured it was raining heavily from 10:00 P.M. until 8:00 A.M. and was rainy

and windy during the daytime. Air conditioning was used occasionally during noontime and afterwards. Site 4, which is located outdoors on the street near the restaurant, showed much temperature stability and had little afternoon fluctuation. Because of the high humidity in the air, wet-bulb and dry-bulb temperatures were very similar. The range of dry-bulb temperature is between 25.2 degrees C (77.5 degrees F) at 6:00 A.M. to 27.6 degrees C (81.5 degrees F) at 8:00 P.M.

Winter temperatures of the four sites in the below-ground restaurant differ from each other in pattern (fig. 95). Site 1 dry-bulb temperature is steady at night and fluctuates from 10:00 A.M. until evening. The fluctuation of the wet-bulb temperatures is similar. The range of dry-bulb temperatures is 14.6 degrees C (58.5 degrees F) at 6:00 A.M. to 18.6 degrees C (65.5 degrees F) in the evening.

Site 2 has a lower temperature than site 1 most of the time and fluctuates greatly in the morning as well as in the evening. The dry-bulb temperature and the wet-bulb temperature are almost parallel to each other during the day and night with a difference of between 2 and 5 degrees C. The minimum dry-bulb temperature is 13.2 degrees C (56 degrees F) in the morning and the maximum of 18.4 degrees C (65 degrees F) at noon. At site 3, dry- and wet-bulb temperatures drop steadily during the night to reach their lowest point at 6:00 A.M. with 4.4 degrees C (40 degrees F) wet-bulb and 5 degrees C (41 degrees F) dry-bulb temperature. They reach their peak at 1:00 P.M. with 12.4 degrees C (54.5 degrees F) dry-bulb and 10.2 wet-bulb. Site 4, the outdoor site located in the street, fluctuates most of the time. The lowest point of dry- and wet-bulb temperatures is at 7:00 A.M. and its highest is at 3:00 P.M. with the dry-bulb at 2.8 degrees C (37 degrees F) and the wet-bulb at 2.2 degrees C (36 degrees F). In any case, sites 1, 2, and 3 would require a little heating in order to bring the ambient temperature to a comfortable level in the winter.

Relative humidity of the below-ground restaurant is detailed in figure 96. In general it shows a very high relative humidity in the summer and a lower relative humidity in the winter, with much differentiation in the below-ground places (sites 1 and 2).

Summer relative humidity in site 1 is more stable during the night and fluctuates throughout the day. Similar patterns developed

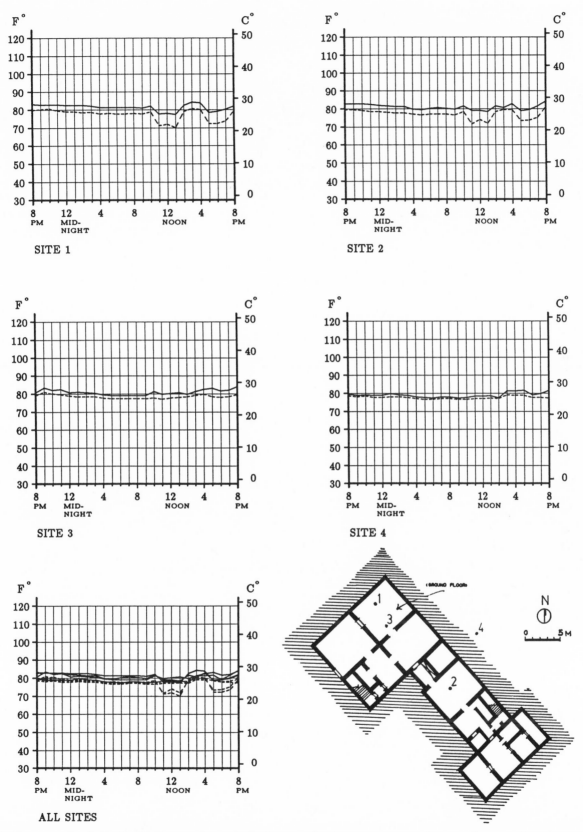

Fig. 94. Summer dry-bulb (solid line) and wet-bulb (broken line) temperatures of an underground restaurant in Shanghai, measured 31 July–1 August 1985. Sites 1 and 2 are in below-ground spaces, site 3 is indoors on the street level, and site 4 is at the side of the street.

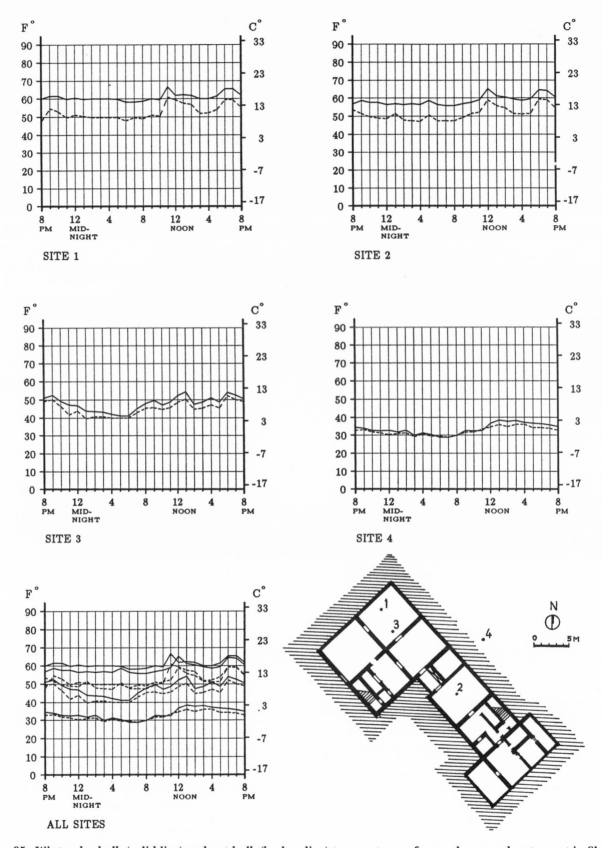

Fig. 95. Winter dry-bulb (solid line) and wet-bulb (broken line) temperatures of an underground restaurant in Shanghai, measured 26–27 December 1984. Sites 1 and 2 are in below-ground spaces, site 3 is indoors on the street
level, and site 4 is at the side of the street.

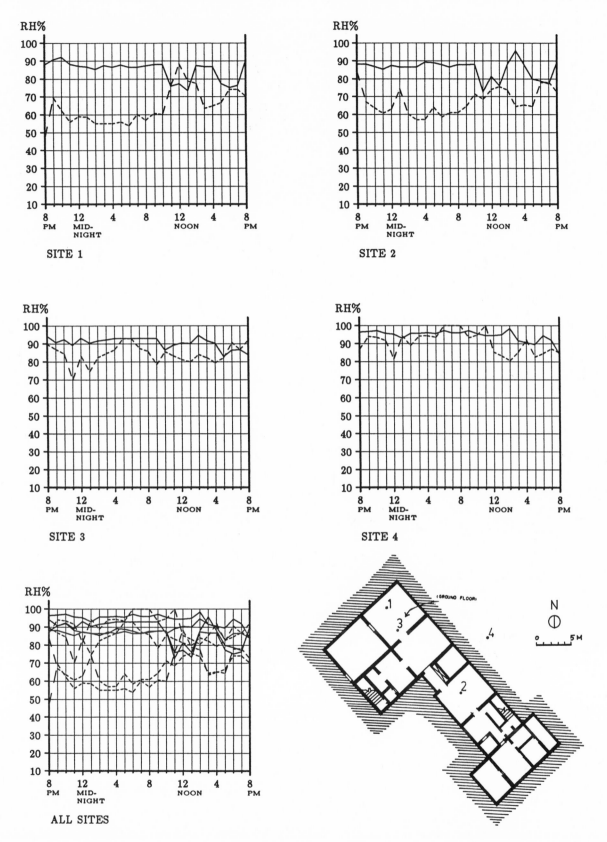

Fig. 96. Summer (solid line) and winter (broken line) relative humidity of the below-ground restaurant in Shanghai.

in sites 2 and 3 as well. In site 1 the relative humidity is in the upper 80s during the night and ranges between a low of 73 percent at 1:00 P.M. to a high of 92 percent at 10:00 P.M. The fluctuation range of below-ground site 2 is much greater in the daytime than it is in site 1. Here in Site 2 the night relative humidity ranges between 86 percent and 89 percent and the day relative humidity ranges from a low of 73 percent at 11:00 A.M. to a high of 96 percent at 3:00 P.M. The outdoor relative humidity of the summer influences site 4. It fluctuates less during the night, with a range of 93 to 97 percent, compared to the daytime with a high of 98 percent at 2:00 P.M. and a low of 86 percent at 8:00 P.M.

The winter relative humidity introduces a different pattern from that of the summer with less diurnal stability. The relative humidity of the winter in site 1 is usually far lower than that of the summer (the 50s compared to the 80s) except for three hours around noon, when it exceeds the summer relative humidity to reach a level of 89 percent. We attribute this to the increase in customers during lunchtime. The below-ground space of site 2 also fluctuates during the night with a range of between 83 percent at 8:00 P.M. to 58 percent at 3:00 A.M. The range of the relative humidity is less in the daytime than it is at night in site 2, with a low of 65 percent between 3:00 and 5:00 P.M. and a high of 79 percent at 6:00 P.M. At the above-ground site 3 the relative humidity ranges between a low of 70 percent at 11:00 P.M. and a high of 94 percent at 6:00 A.M. with much fluctuation during the night and day. The outdoor site 4 has much fluctuation in its relative humidity in the morning when it reaches 100 percent between 6–8:00 A.M. and again at 11:00 A.M. The lower range was 81 percent at midnight and 80 percent at 2:00 P.M. At all sites relative humidity ranged as low as 50 percent in the winter and as high as 100 percent in the summer.

4
Conclusion

Chinese experience in below-ground space usage has become comprehensive during the last three and a half decades. Today usage is diverse and indications are that it will continue to be so in the future. This practice is becoming increasingly employed throughout China in areas beyond the loess soil zone, where it was common in the distant past. This phase of entering new regions outside the loess soil zone necessitates the treatment of different soil and rock and requires new and modern technology. The Chinese are trying to combine the benefits of the old system with modern technology. As their engineers and architects become more knowledgeable, they will enforce this direction in the future.

The need for mechanization of below-ground space excavation is currently a crucial matter for such projects in China. Both residential and nonresidential usage must become more prevalent to reduce the cost of construction. This matter will become more critical as the Chinese begin rock-cutting outside the loess soil zone.

The limitation on mechanization is not only a matter of affordability and knowledge but also a matter of socialization and employment. The use of below-ground space in China will increase, primarily in the nonresidential usage of modern facilities of various types.

The reasons for sophisticated use of below-ground space in China have been apparent throughout history and are evident today as well. Some of these factors are:

1. The cradle of Chinese civilization was in the loess soil region, which covers a major part of northern China.
2. The shortage of building materials, especially of wood for the last several centuries, supports the construction of a traditional underground structure that does not require other building materials.
3. The need for food protection, complicated by the shortage of land suitable for agriculture, led to the need for innovative concepts of housing design and land preservation.
4. Below-ground air, used for cooling in summer and for warmth in winter, results in energy savings.
5. Civil defense needs in large cities during the 1960s led to the conversion of these spaces for public uses such as manufacturing, assembly halls, theaters, classrooms, food storage, and so on.
6. No high or advanced technology is required in the loess soil zone.

Many Chinese workers in factories below-ground favor this environment because it is cool in summer and warm in the winter. The employer, however, must often compensate the employee with higher pay or with shorter working hours because of the limitations of the relatively narrow tunneling of the space.[1]

In any case, in China many economic, tech-

123

nological, and sociocultural forces have led to continuous use of below-ground space. Moreover, the motivation today is beyond economic benefit and is related to solving urban problems such as congestion.

The use of below-ground space is more suitable to Chinese circumstances than it is to those of other developing countries. Chinese society is very cooperative, communally oriented, and complies with pressure from authorities. It seems this old-new movement of below-ground space usage will be accelerated even more in the near future.

In the city, public below-ground space can be used between two above-ground buildings, under parks, or under streets. In any case, the overall plan of the city should introduce above- and below-ground space usage as two integral parts. Public below-ground space should be a pleasing environment in order to attract people to use it and spend much time there.

Through practice, the Chinese have realized the comprehensive benefits of below-ground space for food storage. It is lower in cost by at least one-third when compared with above-ground areas. There is no effect or damage from wind, rain, flood, or fire, and it is protected from insects and birds. It is simple and convenient to construct. In general, below-ground storage is preferable to above-ground storage. Chinese development of below-ground food storage facilities, especially for grain, has achieved a high standard. Combining ancient experience with modern knowledge in this field has brought recognition to China, which is considered one of the leading countries in the world, if not the leading one, in developing successful underground storage. This experience is especially noteworthy for developing countries, where food shortages and famine still constitute major threats to physical survival.

The design details of the underground space environment will determine the overall attitude of the user. This interior design should start from the outdoors, at the entrance, and should create a tranquil and inviting environment. The feeling of a lack of space and the elimination of the common perception of claustrophobia can be diminished by a variety of design elements that address psychological and practical needs. Space, especially for public gatherings, should be wide and have high ceilings generous enough to establish the feeling of comfort and eliminate the common feeling of confinement. Color is an-

other essential element that contributes to an overall mood. It should be light such as white, light beige, blue, and the like. Moreover, special attention should be given to the transition between outdoors and indoors. Any element associated with the traditional negative bias concerning below-ground space (such as darkness or dim light, dampness, or moisture) should be eliminated.

Two major principles should be adopted by a designer of below-ground space in order to minimize or eliminate this claustrophobia. If possible, the entrance to the below-ground space should be ascending rather than descending. This can be accomplished in hilly or mountainous areas where cliffs are available. Second, if possible, the user should be able to look directly outdoors. Such contact will bring inside the cycle of nature, the movement of birds, wind, trees, and of people and establish a relationship between the user and the outdoor environment. Such a design is also more possible in a hilly, rolling, or mountainous area.

If achieving these two principles is not possible because of a flat site, then it becomes essential to improve the interior environment through the use of common interior design techniques. In addition to the color and size considerations already discussed, light should be generously supplied and resemble outdoor light as much as possible, as for instance, fluorescent light does. Another element to be introduced into the interior underground space is vegetation, especially the kind that does not require bright light. Paintings of landscapes can also be introduced. Of course, with modern technology one can create an illusion of eye contact with the outdoor environment by using a video camera to project outdoor scenes onto a screen. Air circulation is one of the most important elements that must be considered in a below-ground environment. Air movement is needed not only for health and hygiene, but also to establish subconscious contact with the outdoor world.

All in all, the design of below-ground space for public gatherings necessitates a comprehensive treatment from an interdisciplinary team rather than the traditional treatment of an engineer-architect. The sociopsychological aspect is equally important to the engineering consideration of below-ground space. This is true in below-ground educational and entertainment environments as well as in the working and production environment.

In summary, the attitude of the below-ground user is determined by both psychological and physiological needs. The latter is determined by thermal comfort and by relative humidity. In general, although the comfort index varies for different people, it is commonly within the range of 18 to 22 degrees C (64.5 to 72 degrees F). The range of 55 to 65 percent relative humidity is also considered acceptable to most people. Some scientists determine the comfort index by adding the dry-bulb temperature to the wet-bulb temperature and dividing the sum by two.

Chinese standards of living and housing are considerably different from those of Western society. Also, the design and performance standards for below-ground space are different from comparable above-ground space in China. Chinese below-ground dwellings are deficient in ventilation, have poor lighting, are subject to low air quality and high humidity, have problems with condensation during warm and rainy seasons, and present fire and safety hazards by comparison to Western requirements. Historically, Chinese residential below-ground space evolved through practice and experimentation, most often being built privately, and as a result it was not preconceived in the modern planning sense. Through this practical experience the Chinese accumulated more than four thousand years of knowledge. On the other hand, nonresidential below-ground space has most commonly been initiated, planned, executed, and maintained by the government, which has drawn extensively on historical traditions. The ability of the Chinese to take initiative, be pragmatic, and create a sense of balance in their environment found expression in these traditions. However, the centralized power structure of the contemporary Communist government has weakened these elements by standardizing many such aspects of Chinese life. In any case, the use of urban nonresidential below-ground space arose from historical experience, existing geopolitical conditions, land shortages within existing urban areas (especially in the larger cities), the readiness of the Chinese to innovate, and their strong motivation to make improvements.

The estimated thirty to forty million Chinese living below ground reside in dwellings confined to the loess soil (the most suitable for this type of dwelling) of five provinces in northern China. Modern development of urban nonresidential below-ground space is not confined to the loess soil alone, but extends throughout most large cities in China mainly because of the construction of massive civil defense shelters in the 1950s. During the last two decades there has been a movement to converting these spaces to public uses and this has intensified interest in the uses for and applications of below-ground space. Almost all these nonresidential below-ground spaces consume more energy for lighting than those above ground, have limited ventilation, and require improved air quality. We observed that below-ground space cut into rock, such as those in Beijing and Chongqing, has lower humidity and condensation in the summer than similar below-ground spaces cut into the loess soil. This may be a result of the greater depth of urban nonresidential below-ground space (10 to 30 meters) in comparison to the depth of the loess soil dwellings (8 to 10 meters). Rock-cut, below-ground space is wider, higher, longer, and has at least two open ends (linear tunneling network). This results in lower humidity and less moisture condensation. Although modern urban nonresidential below-ground spaces are planned, it is necessary that more thought be given to planning for utilities and performance in order to bring them up to Western standards. This is especially true of the hundreds of kilometers of civil defense shelters that have been converted to public uses, and less so of the modern below-ground developments that are planned, designed, and used for specific purposes.

Nevertheless, new uses of urban nonresidential below-ground space in the 1970s and 1980s in China respond positively to growing urban land use problems. These uses also meet Chinese criteria for relatively low expenditures on urban development. It is essential to understand that in spite of the rigid Chinese policies for control of urban growth, existing congested urban land-use patterns in Chinese cities have created acute problems for the last decade, especially now that China has been opened to Western modernization and reform. Equally important are the relatively rapid changes taking place in the living standards of urban Chinese and the extreme space limitations of Chinese residential buildings, which will have implications for the consumption of below-ground space. These changes and limitations have accentuated the need for the development of new land uses for entertainment and cultural activities (especially for Chinese youth), modern shopping facilities, central urban open spaces (such as recreational areas), and last for the requirements of modern transportation.

Finally, to the best of our knowledge, the danger of radon contamination was not an issue during the course of our field research in China. There had not been any research conducted on radon in China, nor was it discussed in the Chinese literature. Our questions about radon revealed a limited awareness of this subject among the Chinese.

Appendix 1
Chronology of Chinese Dynasties

Xia	c. 21st-century–16th-century B.C.	Southern Dynasties	420–589
		Song	420–479
Shang	c. 16th-century–11th-century B.C.	Qi	479–502
		Liang	502-557
Zhou	c. 11th century–221 B.C.	Chen	557–589
Western Zhou	c. 11th century–770 B.C.	Northern Dynasties	386–581
		Northern Wei	386–534
Eastern Zhou	770–221 B.C.	Western Wei	535–557
Spring and Autumn Period	770–476 B.C.	Northern Qi	550–577
		Northern Zhou	557–581
Warring States Period	475–221 B.C.	Sui	581–618
Qin	221–207 B.C.	Tang	618–907
Han	206 B.C.–A.D. 220	Five Dynasties and Ten Kingdoms	907–979
Western Han	206 B.C.–A.D. 24		
Eastern Han	25–220	Song	960–1279
Three Kingdoms	220–230	Northern Song	960–1127
Wei	220–265	Southern Song	1127–1279
Shu	221–263	Liao	916–1125
Wu	222–280	Kin	1115–1234
Jin	265–420	Yuan	1271–1368
Western Jin	265–316	Ming	1368–1644
Eastern Jin	317–420	Qing	1644–1911
Southern and Northern Dynasties	420–589		

Source: China Facts and Figures: 4,000-Year History (Beijing: Foreign Languages Press, 1982), 7.

Appendix 2
Statistical Tables

Diurnal Temperature Measurements in Shanghai

Workers Hospital

Summer
Aug 1-2, 1985

Degrees in Centigrade

Time	SITES								1	2	
	1		2		3		4				
	Dry	Wet	Dry	Wet	Dry	Wet	Dry	Wet	Persons		Weather
8:00 pm	27.0	24.4	27.0	24.6	27.2	24.8	26.8	24.4	6	3	AC - Cloudy
9:00	26.8	24.2	26.6	24.0	27.4	24.6	26.6	24.8	6	3	AC - Cloudy
10:00	27.0	24.2	26.8	24.2	27.6	24.4	26.8	25.0	6	3	No wind,clear
11:00	27.0	24.2	26.6	24.0	27.0	25.0	26.4	25.2	6	3	No wind,clear
Midnight	26.8	24.2	26.6	23.8	27.0	24.8	26.2	25.6	6	3	No wind,clear
1:00 am	26.8	24.0	26.6	23.8	26.8	24.6	26.4	26.0	6	3	No wind,clear
2:00	26.8	24.0	26.6	23.8	26.8	26.0	26.2	26.0	6	3	No wind,clear
3:00	26.6	23.8	26.4	23.6	26.8	24.4	26.2	26.0	6	3	No wind,clear
4:00	26.6	24.0	26.6	23.8	27.0	24.6	26.2	25.9	6	3	No wind,clear
5:00	26.4	23.8	26.4	23.6	26.8	24.2	26.2	25.8	6	3	No wind,clear
6:00	26.6	24.0	26.4	23.8	26.8	24.4	26.2	26.0	6	3	No wind,clear
7:00	26.8	24.4	26.6	23.8	26.8	24.4	28.0	26.8	6	3	No wind,clear
8:00	26.4	23.9	26.6	23.9	26.8	24.4	28.8	27.1	6	3	No wind,clear
9:00	26.8	24.2	26.6	23.9	27.2	25.2	31.4	27.4	6	3	No wind,clear
10:00	26.7	24.2	26.4	23.7	27.0	24.8	31.5	27.4	5	2	No wind,clear
11:00	26.6	24.2	26.2	23.8	27.0	24.6	32.5	28.5	5	2	No wind,clear
Noon	26.8	24.2	26.4	23.8	26.9	24.6	31.9	28.1	6	3	No wind,clear
1:00 pm	26.9	24.2	26.6	23.9	26.9	24.6	31.9	28.0	6	3	No wind,clear
2:00	26.9	24.4	26.6	24.0	26.9	25.2	29.2	26.6	6	1	Wind,cloudy
3:00	26.6	24.2	26.4	24.0	26.8	24.4	27.8	24.6	3	1	Wind,cloudy
4:00	26.8	24.6	26.6	23.7	26.9	24.4	28.2	25.6	5	4	Wind,cloudy
5:00	26.8	24.2	26.6	23.7	26.9	24.6	29.0	26.7	5	4	Wind,cloudy
6:00	26.6	24.1	26.8	24.2	27.0	24.6	29.6	27.2	4	0	Wind,cloudy
7:00	26.6	24.0	26.8	24.0	27.1	24.2	28.6	26.8	6	3	Wind,cloudy
8:00	26.4	24.0	26.6	24.0	27.2	24.2	28.2	26.5	6	3	Wind,cloudy

Diurnal Temperature Measurements in Shanghai

Workers Hospital

Winter
Dec 22-23,1984

Degrees in Centigrade

Time	SITES								No. of Persons	
	1		2		3		4		site 1	site 2
	Dry	Wet	Dry	Wet	Dry	Wet	Dry	Wet		
8:00 pm	17.6	11.2	17.6	11.0	15.8	10.2	-1.6	-3.6	9	11
9:00	17.2	15.2	17.6	15.4	15.8	14.4	-1.6	-3.5	7	10
10:00	17.0	14.0	17.0	14.0	16.6	13.2	-2.0	-4.0	7	10
11:00	16.8	13.6	17.0	15.4	15.6	12.6	-2.2	-2.1	6	11
Midnight	17.2	13.6	17.0	15.4	15.6	12.6	-2.2	-2.3	8	11
1:00 am	18.0	13.2	17.6	12.6	15.6	12.4	-2.4	-4.2	8	11
2:00	18.2	13.6	18.0	13.4	15.6	11.4	-2.8	-2.9	8	11
3:00	18.0	13.8	18.2	13.4	15.4	11.4	-2.6	-4.8	8	11
4:00	18.0	13.8	18.2	13.6	15.4	11.4	-2.8	-4.0	8	11
5:00	18.2	13.8	17.8	13.0	15.9	11.4	-2.8	-5.0	8	11
6:00	17.4	13.0	18.2	12.4	15.4	11.6	-2.8	-3.0	8	11
7:00	17.2	12.6	17.1	12.2	16.2	12.2	-2.8	-3.0	5	8
8:00	16.9	11.8	17.1	13.2	15.3	11.4	-1.8	-2.0	4	9
9:00	17.2	11.2	15.3	11.0	15.4	10.9	-1.6	-2.8	8	10
10:00	17.0	10.6	17.2	10.2	14.8	11.5	-1.1	-1.6	5	8
11:00	17.2	10.3	16.2	10.0	14.2	11.3	-0.4	-1.3	5	8
Noon	17.4	10.5	16.6	9.8	14.3	10.8	-0.5	-1.8	4	8
1:00 pm	17.1	10.4	16.8	11.0	14.5	10.6	-0.8	-1.6	5	7
2:00	17.2	11.2	17.0	10.8	14.9	11.0	-0.8	-1.8	10	9
3:00	17.2	11.2	15.4	10.2	15.2	11.0	0.2	-1.7	5	7
4:00	17.4	11.2	16.6	10.0	14.8	10.8	-0.4	-1.8	6	7
5:00	17.2	11.0	16.5	10.2	15.0	10.9	-0.4	-1.4	5	6
6:00	17.2	11.0	17.0	11.2	15.0	10.6	-0.4	-2.5	12	6
7:00	17.0	10.8	16.4	10.4	15.4	10.6	-0.2	-3.2	6	11
8:00	17.0	10.8	16.8	10.8	15.2	10.4	-0.1	-3.2	6	15

Relative Humidity Calculations

Workers Hospital   Summer

Time	SITES			
	1	2	3	4
	RH%	RH%	RH%	RH%
8:00 pm	96.9	83.7	84.1	84.0
9:00	95.7	82.9	81.4	87.9
10:00	94.2	82.6	79.4	87.9
11:00	81.3	82.9	86.5	91.5
Midnight	82.6	81.5	85.1	95.7
1:00 am	81.5	81.5	85.1	97.2
2:00	81.5	81.5	94.6	98.8
3:00	81.5	81.1	98.4	98.8
4:00	82.9	81.5	83.7	98.0
5:00	82.5	81.1	82.6	97.2
6:00	82.9	82.5	84.0	98.8
7:00	84.0	81.5	84.0	91.7
8:00	83.2	82.2	84.0	88.6
9:00	82.6	82.2	86.6	75.9
10:00	83.3	81.8	85.1	75.3
11:00	83.9	83.8	83.7	76.2
Noon	82.6	82.5	84.4	76.9
1:00 pm	81.9	82.2	84.4	76.6
2:00	83.3	82.9	88.3	83.2
3:00	83.9	83.9	84.0	79.1
4:00	85.1	80.8	83.3	83.0
5:00	82.6	80.8	84.4	84.9
6:00	83.2	82.6	83.7	84.7
7:00	82.9	81.5	80.9	88.3
8:00	83.9	82.9	80.3	88.9

Relative Humidity Calculations

Workers Hospital   Winter

Time	SITES			
	1	**2**	**3**	**4**
	RH%	RH%	RH%	RH%
8:00 pm	141.7	54.1	56.4	63.5
9:00	187.7	82.6	88.2	72.5
10:00	188.1	75.0	72.9	65.5
11:00	185.5	82.6	75.3	133.8
Midnight	173.6	68.8	66.5	138.1
1:00 am	160.8	65.6	74.0	70:1
2:00	163.4	68.0	66.5	142.5
3:00	168.9	65.2	66.5	69.3
4:00	168.9	65.3	66.5	78.6
5:00	166.4	63.9	64.3	66.9
6:00	167.9	57.6	68.8	150.6
7:00	165.3	62.6	68.2	154.1
8:00	159.1	69.6	68.3	160.5
9:00	147.1	65.4	63.9	81.9
10:00	141.7	48.7	72.7	92.6
11:00	136.0	53.0	75.4	87.4
Noon	135.8	49.4	70.6	81.2
1:00 pm	138.9	56.2	67.3	88.7
2:00	147.1	53.5	68.0	85.6
3:00	147.1	58.7	66.2	79.2
4:00	144.0	50.8	67.1	80.5
5:00	145.0	52.2	66.5	85.8
6:00	145.0	56.1	64.0	71.6
7:00	144.5	55.5	61.5	59.7
8:00	144.5	54.8	61.7	58.5

Diurnal Temperature Measurements in Shanghai

Furniture Exhibition Hall

Summer
Aug 2-3,1985

Degrees in Centigrade

Time	SITES								NOTES
	1		2		3		4		
	Dry	Wet	Dry	Wet	Dry	Wet	Dry	Wet	
8:00 pm	28.0	24.4	27.6	24.4	27.8	24.8	28.0	26.8	Cloudy
9:00	27.8	24.4	27.4	24.8	27.4	25.6	27.6	26.2	Cloudy
10:00	27.8	25.4	27.4	25.0	27.4	25.6	27.4	26.0	Fan in 2 - Cloudy
11:00	28.0	25.2	27.2	25.2	27.4	25.4	27.1	25.8	Fan in 2 - Cloudy
Midnight	27.6	25.0	27.6	25.0	27.2	25.2	27.1	25.4	No Fan in 2 - Cloudy
1:00 am	27.8	25.2	27.4	25.2	27.0	24.8	26.8	25.4	No Fan in 2 - Cloudy
2:00	27.8	25.1	27.6	25.0	27.0	24.8	26.4	25.2	2 persons in 2 - Part. Cloudy
3:00	27.6	25.0	27.6	25.2	27.0	24.8	26.2	25.0	2 persons in 2 - Windy,clear
4:00	27.6	25.0	27.4	25.0	27.0	24.8	26.2	25.0	Windy,clear
5:00	27.6	25.2	27.4	25.0	26.8	24.8	26.2	24.8	Clear
6:00	27.6	25.2	27.4	25.0	26.8	24.6	26.4	24.8	Clear
7:00	27.6	25.2	27.2	25.0	26.8	24.6	26.8	25.2	Cloudy
8:00	28.2	25.0	28.4	24.4	27.0	24.9	27.8	25.8	Dehumidifier, Cloudy
9:00	28.4	24.0	28.8	24.6	27.4	25.2	28.2	26.0	Cloudy
10:00	28.8	24.2	28.6	25.4	27.8	25.2	28.6	25.6	Cloudy
11:00	28.6	24.8	28.6	24.0	27.6	24.4	28.6	25.4	Cloudy
Noon	29.0	24.4	29.0	23.6	27.8	23.8	28.9	25.6	Cloudy
1:00 pm	29.2	24.4	29.2	23.2	27.8	24.0	29.2	25.4	Drizzling
2:00	28.4	23.6	28.9	23.2	27.4	24.0	29.4	25.8	Drizzling
3:00	28.6	23.8	28.4	23.2	27.4	24.0	31.0	26.8	Clear
4:00	28.2	24.0	28.4	23.2	28.0	24.0	31.8	25.8	Clear
5:00	28.4	23.8	28.6	23.2	27.8	23.8	31.0	25.4	Clear
6:00	28.2	24.0	28.4	23.8	27.8	24.4	30.0	25.0	Clear
7:00	28.4	24.2	28.6	24.6	27.8	24.6	29.0	26.2	Clear
8:00	27.9	24.6	28.2	24.6	27.1	24.8	28.4	26.0	Clear

Diurnal Temperature Measurements in Shanghai

Furniture Exhibition Hall

Winter
Dec 23-24,1984

Degrees in Centigrade

Time	SITES								No. of Persons			
	1		2		3		4		Sites			
	Dry	Wet	Dry	Wet	Dry	Wet	Dry	Wet	1	2	3	
8:00 pm	13.4	5.2	14.2	8.0	15.2	8.8	-1.2	-1.6	4	2	2	
9:00	13.6	9.4	14.4	8.8	14.6	9.4	-1.4	-1.6	4	2	2	
10:00	13.2	8.0	14.0	7.4	15.2	8.0	-1.0	-1.4	3	2	2	
11:00	13.2	8.2	14.0	7.0	15.0	7.0	-1.8	-2.4	2	2	2	
Midnight	17.4	12.6	14.2	6.8	15.2	7.4	-2.2	-3.4	1	1	1	
1:00 am	14.2	8.0	9.6	7.4	15.4	7.6	-2.4	-2.8	1	1	1	
2:00	14.0	7.8	9.4	7.2	15.2	7.4	-3.0	-4.0	1	1	1	
3:00	13.6	8.4	15.6	7.8	15.4	7.0	-2.4	-3.4	1	1	2	
4:00	11.6	6.6	14.2	6.8	15.4	7.0	-3.6	-4.6	2	2	2	
5:00	13.2	8.2	14.8	7.6	15.4	7.2	-4.0	-4.4	1	2	2	
6:00	13.2	7.6	14.4	7.2	15.4	7.6	-4.2	-4.4	2	2	2	
7:00	13.0	7.4	14.2	6.6	14.8	7.4	-4.2	-4.8	3	3	1	
8:00	11.8	7.6	13.4	6.2	14.8	7.6	-3.8	-3.9	1	2	1	
9:00	11.6	7.9	13.2	6.4	14.8	7.4	-2.8	-3.0	2	1	4	
10:00	15.4	9.6	12.8	9.4	15.4	7.6	-0.2	-0.8	1	4	3	
11:00	11.4	7.4	12.2	7.2	15.2	7.6	-0.2	-0.8	1	1	1	
Noon	11.4	7.4	12.0	7.1	14.8	7.0	-0.2	-0.8	1	1	1	
1:00 pm	11.4	7.0	11.8	7.2	14.8	6.8	-0.2	-0.6	1	2	3	
2:00	11.4	6.4	11.2	6.4	15.0	6.8	-0.2	-0.6	1	7	1	
3:00	11.2	6.8	12.4	8.0	15.2	7.0	0.6	-1.0	1	6	1	
4:00	11.6	6.8	12.4	7.4	15.6	7.0	1.0	-0.8	1	1	1	
5:00	12.0	7.2	12.4	7.8	15.2	7.0	0.0	-2.5	2	2	1	
6:00	12.9	7.1	13.4	8.1	15.4	9.0	-0.8	-2.5	2	2	1	
7:00	13.0	7.4	12.8	8.2	15.2	8.4	-0.8	-2.5	1	1	1	
8:00	13.0	7.4	12.8	8.2	15.2	9.1	-1.0	-2.5	1	1	1	

Relative Humidity Calculations

Furniture Exhibition Hall   Summer

Time	SITES			
	1	2	3	4
	RH%	RH%	RH%	RH%
8:00 pm	76.9	79.4	80.5	91.7
9:00	78.1	82.8	87.7	90.6
10:00	84.2	84.1	87.7	90.6
11:00	81.6	86.6	86.6	91.3
Midnight	83.1	83.1	80.3	88.7
1:00 am	82.9	85.2	85.1	90.5
2:00	82.2	83.1	85.1	91.5
3:00	83.1	84.2	85.1	91.9
4:00	83.1	84.1	85.1	90.4
5:00	84.2	84.1	86.5	88.9
6:00	84.2	84.1	85.1	88.9
7:00	84.2	85.5	85.1	89.0
8:00	79.6	74.8	85.8	86.7
9:00	71.7	73.6	85.2	85.7
10:00	71.4	79.7	82.9	80.7
11:00	76.1	71.7	79.4	79.7
Noon	71.5	67.0	74.5	78.8
1:00 pm	70.7	64.1	75.8	76.3
2:00	70.0	65.4	78.0	77.4
3:00	70.4	67.9	78.0	74.5
4:00	73.7	67.9	74.6	65.4
5:00	70.4	67.0	74.5	67.1
6:00	73.7	71.3	78.1	69.8
7:00	73.5	74.8	79.1	81.8
8:00	78.5	76.9	84.8	84.4

Relative Humidity Calculations

Furniture Exhibition Hall   Winter

Time	SITES			
	1	**2**	**3**	**4**
	RH%	RH%	RH%	RH%
8:00 pm	35.4	50.7	50.3	94.2
9:00	64.8	55.2	58.3	112.7
10:00	56.8	47.3	45.1	105.7
11:00	58.0	44.6	39.4	121.8
Midnight	63.2	35.6	41.1	81.5
1:00 am	50.7	78.8	41.1	93.9
2:00	50.1	78.2	47.7	84.2
3:00	57.2	66.1	37.5	84.6
4:00	56.2	35.6	37.5	83.8
5:00	58.0	44.2	38.6	92.6
6:00	53.5	43.7	41.1	96.2
7:00	53.3	40.7	43.1	89.7
8:00	62.7	42.2	44.2	120.8
9:00	67.1	45.0	43.1	116.2
10:00	54.7	70.4	41.1	91.3
11:00	64.1	56.9	42.2	91.3
Noon	64.1	57.2	40.5	91.3
1:00 pm	60.9	61.3	39.1	94.4
2:00	56.0	57.5	38.0	94.4
3:00	60.7	62.0	38.6	79.6
4:00	58.0	57.2	36.7	76.7
5:00	58.0	60.2	38.6	66.4
6:00	51.5	55.8	50.6	76.4
7:00	53.3	60.6	47.7	76.4
8:00	53.3	60.6	52.2	78.5

Diurnal Temperature Measurements in Shanghai

Department Store No. 9

Summer
Aug 4-5,1985

Degrees in Centigrade

Time	SITES								NOTES	
	1		2		3		4		site 1	site 4
	Dry	Wet	Dry	Wet	Dry	Wet	Dry	Wet		
8:00 pm	28.8	26.0	29.0	26.0	28.8	26.3	28.2	26.0	Fan	Cloudy
9:00	28.8	26.2	29.2	26.4	28.9	26.4	28.0	26.6	Fan	Cloudy
10:00	28.8	26.2	29.0	26.4	29.0	26.8	28.4	26.8	Fan	Cloudy
11:00	28.6	26.3	29.1	26.6	29.0	26.9	27.8	26.6	Fan	Clear
Midnight	28.6	26.0	29.0	26.4	28.9	26.6	27.2	26.0	Fan	Clear
1:00 am	28.6	26.0	29.0	26.2	28.4	26.4	27.0	25.8	Fan	Clear
2:00	28.4	26.0	29.0	26.4	28.4	26.2	27.0	25.6	Fan	Clear
3:00	28.6	26.0	28.8	26.2	28.4	26.2	27.0	25.6	Fan	Clear
4:00	28.6	25.8	28.8	26.0	28.2	26.2	26.4	25.2	Fan	Clear
5:00	28.6	25.9	28.7	26.0	28.2	26.2	26.8	25.6	Fan	Clear
6:00	28.4	25.8	28.8	26.2	28.1	26.2	27.4	26.0	Fan	Clear
7:00	28.4	25.8	28.8	26.0	28.6	27.0	28.6	26.4	Fan	Clear
8:00	28.8	25.9	28.8	25.8	28.6	25.9	29.0	26.2	Fan	Clear
9:00	28.6	25.8	28.9	26.2	29.4	26.6	31.0	29.0	many people	Clear
10:00	28.6	25.6	28.9	26.4	30.0	26.6	30.9	27.1	many people	Clear
11:00	28.6	25.5	29.0	26.0	30.6	26.9	30.6	27.8	many people	
Noon	29.6	26.4	29.6	26.6	30.6	27.2	30.7	27.6	many people	
1:00 pm	29.4	26.2	30.0	27.0	30.8	27.2	31.2	27.4	many people	
2:00	29.2	26.2	29.4	26.2	31.6	27.4	32.4	27.6	many people	
3:00	28.8	25.8	29.6	26.2	31.8	27.6	32.0	27.8	many people	
4:00	29.4	27.8	29.6	26.4	31.6	27.6	31.6	27.4	many people	
5:00	29.6	28.0	30.0	26.8	31.4	27.4	31.3	27.2	many people	
6:00	29.6	28.0	29.8	26.6	31.0	26.8	31.0	26.7	many people	
7:00	29.2	27.3	29.7	26.1	30.4	26.6	30.2	26.4	No Fan	
8:00	29.0	27.0	29.0	26.0	29.9	26.5	29.8	26.4	No Fan	

Air conditioning was on all 24 hours in sites 1, and 2.

Diurnal Temperature Measurements in Shanghai

Department Store No. 9

Winter
Dec 25-26,1984

Degrees in Centigrade

Time	SITES								No. of Persons			
	1		2		3		4		Sites			
	Dry	Wet	Dry	Wet	Dry	Wet	Dry	Wet	1	2	3	
8:00 pm	13.4	9.0	12.0	6.6	7.4	4.4	1.4	0.4				
9:00	13.6	9.4	11.6	6.6	6.8	4.0	1.0	0.4				
10:00	13.8	9.2	11.6	6.6	5.6	3.6	0.2	0.0				
11:00	13.4	8.8	12.2	6.2	5.6	3.4	0.2	-0.4				
Midnight	13.6	8.8	10.8	6.2	5.6	3.6	0.2	-0.4				
1:00 am	13.2	8.8	11.0	6.6	5.6	3.4	0.2	-0.4				
2:00	13.2	8.6	10.8	6.6	5.6	3.6	0.4	0.4				
3:00	13.2	8.8	11.4	6.4	5.4	3.2	-0.4	-1.4				
4:00	13.6	8.6	10.8	6.4	5.4	3.2	-0.8	-1.0				
5:00	13.6	9.8	10.6	6.4	5.2	3.0	-1.0	-1.8				
6:00	13.8	8.6	10.8	6.6	5.2	3.2	-1.2	-2.4				
7:00	13.4	8.4	10.6	5.6	5.0	3.0	1.0	-1.6	2	2	2	
8:00	13.2	9.0	11.8	6.4	4.6	3.2	1.2	-0.8	2	2	14	
9:00	13.2	10.8	11.5	6.6	7.6	6.2	1.2	-0.8	16	15		
10:00	13.8	9.0	11.4	6.2	8.0	5.5	1.4	-0.2	21	20		
11:00	13.2	8.6	11.6	6.2	7.6	4.8	1.2	0.8	18	8		
Noon	12.0	7.0	12.6	9.2	7.4	5.2	3.0	1.2	17	11		
1:00 pm	14.2	10.6	11.8	6.5	7.4	4.8	4.2	1.6	18	9		
2:00	13.8	9.4	12.2	7.0	8.2	5.2	4.0	1.4	16	27		
3:00	13.6	9.4	12.8	7.6	9.2	5.4	3.6	1.2	19	27		
4:00	14.0	10.6	12.8	7.8	9.0	6.2	2.8	1.4	32	19		
5:00	13.8	10.2	12.6	7.8	7.6	5.6	2.0	0.4	18	10		
6:00	13.4	9.6	12.4	7.6	8.0	6.1	2.4	1.0	12	12		
7:00	13.2	8.4	12.2	8.0	6.8	4.2	2.4	1.1	2	2		
8:00	13.2	8.4	11.2	7.5	6.9	3.8	1.4	0.4	2	2		

Relative Humidity Calculations

Department Store No. 9   Summer

Time	SITES			
	1	2	3	4
	RH%	RH%	RH%	RH%
8:00 pm	82.1	80.8	83.8	85.7
9:00	83.1	82.2	83.8	90.3
10:00	83.1	83.2	85.6	89.3
11:00	85.1	83.9	86.3	91.7
Midnight	83.4	83.2	84.9	92.0
1:00 am	83.4	81.8	86.8	91.6
2:00	84.4	83.2	85.4	90.1
3:00	83.4	83.1	85.4	90.1
4:00	82.1	82.1	86.8	91.5
5:00	82.7	82.8	86.8	91.6
6:00	83.0	83.1	87.5	90.6
7:00	83.0	82.1	89.7	85.8
8:00	81.4	80.8	82.7	81.8
9:00	82.1	82.5	82.0	87.3
10:00	80.7	81.5	78.5	76.6
11:00	80.4	80.8	77.4	82.6
Noon	80.0	81.0	79.0	80.7
1:00 pm	79.6	81.1	77.8	77.0
2:00	80.9	79.6	75.0	71.7
3:00	80.8	78.7	74.8	74.9
4:00	88.4	80.0	75.9	75.0
5:00	89.8	79.8	75.9	75.2
6:00	89.8	79.8	74.5	73.9
7:00	87.7	78.1	76.4	76.7
8:00	86.9	80.8	78.8	78.8

Relative Humidity Calculations

Department Store No. 9   Winter

Time	SITES			
	1	**2**	**3**	**4**
	RH%	RH%	RH%	RH%
8:00 pm	62.9	53.3	69.2	86.9
9:00	64.8	56.2	70.8	91.8
10:00	61.6	56.2	77.8	97.6
11:00	61.2	49.3	76.0	91.7
Midnight	60.1	58.4	77.8	91.7
1:00 am	62.7	60.1	76.0	91.7
2:00	61.0	61.7	77.8	88.9
3:00	62.7	56.0	75.3	85.8
4:00	58.5	60.3	75.3	97.5
5:00	60.1	61.9	75.7	87.9
6:00	57.0	61.7	77.5	82.2
7:00	58.3	55.0	77.4	67.0
8:00	64.5	53.4	83.9	74.9
9:00	78.9	56.6	85.4	74.9
10:00	60.4	54.2	74.6	80.2
11:00	61.0	53.1	71.5	84.7
Noon	56.7	70.2	76.9	77.7
1:00 pm	69.6	54.3	73.0	70.0
2:00	63.3	54.2	69.9	69.8
3:00	64.8	51.7	63.8	71.8
4:00	70.8	57.6	72.2	82.9
5:00	69.3	59.1	79.2	79.6
6:00	67.3	58.5	80.0	82.6
7:00	59.7	63.5	72.5	83.3
8:00	59.7	66.7	67.6	86.9

Diurnal Temperature Measurements in Shanghai

Workers Club

Summer
Aug 3-4,1985

Degrees in Centigrade

Time	SITES								NOTES
	1		2		3		4		
	Dry	Wet	Dry	Wet	Dry	Wet	Dry	Wet	
8:00 pm	29.6	26.9	29.2	27.0	28.6	26.9	27.8	26.6	180 dancing in # 1,2
9:00	29.4	27.4	29.4	27.2	28.4	27.0	27.6	26.5	230 dancing in # 1,2
10:00	29.0	27.0	29.4	27.2	27.8	26.2	27.3	26.5	230 dancing in # 1,2
11:00	28.1	26.6	27.9	26.4	27.0	25.8	27.2	26.6	0 dancing
Midnight	27.8	26.6	27.8	26.3	27.2	26.0	27.2	26.4	0 dancing
1:00 am	27.8	26.8	27.8	26.4	27.1	25.9	27.0	26.3	0 dancing
2:00	27.9	26.8	27.8	26.3	26.8	25.8	27.2	26.4	0 dancing
3:00	27.9	26.8	27.8	26.3	27.0	25.8	27.0	26.2	0 dancing
4:00	27.8	26.4	27.8	26.4	27.1	25.9	26.8	26.2	Clear
5:00	28.0	26.6	27.6	26.2	27.1	25.8	26.6	25.9	Clear
6:00	27.8	26.4	27.6	26.1	26.8	25.6	27.1	26.2	Clear
7:00	28.0	26.6	27.8	26.2	26.8	25.8	28.0	27.0	Clear
8:00	28.2	26.8	27.8	26.4	27.6	26.0	29.2	27.6	Dehumidifier in # 3
9:00	28.6	27.0	28.2	26.4	27.8	26.2	30.4	28.0	Dehumidifier in # 3
10:00	28.4	26.8	28.4	26.6	28.0	26.4	31.0	28.0	Dehumidifier in # 3
11:00	28.2	26.8	28.0	26.4	28.0	26.4	31.8	28.0	
Noon	28.2	26.9	28.0	26.6	28.0	26.4	32.2	29.0	
1:00 pm	28.2	26.8	28.0	26.6	28.0	26.4	33.0	29.0	
2:00	29.8	28.2	29.4	27.8	28.4	27.2	33.6	29.0	250 in #2 - Clear
3:00	30.2	28.4	29.8	28.0	28.4	27.2	32.2	28.8	250 in #2 - Clear
4:00	29.3	27.4	29.0	28.2	27.6	27.4	31.0	28.3	150 in #2 - Cloudy
5:00	28.6	26.8	28.9	26.0	28.0	26.0	26.0	25.2	150 in #2 - Rainy
6:00	27.8	25.2	27.6	24.9	26.9	25.0	27.4	25.8	0 in #2 - Cloudy
7:00	27.8	25.2	28.0	25.4	30.4	26.2	27.0	25.6	80 in #2 - Clear,Dehumidifie
8:00	29.4	27.4	29.6	27.6	32.2	27.8	28.0	26.0	250 dancing - Dehumidifier

Air conditioning was on all 24 hours in sites 1, 2, and 3.

Diurnal Temperature Measurements in Shanghai

Workers Club

Winter
Dec 24-25,1984

Degrees in Centigrade

Time	SITES								No. of Persons
	1		2		3		4		sites 1,2,3
	Dry	Wet	Dry	Wet	Dry	Wet	Dry	Wet	
8:00 pm	14.6	8.4	15.2	11.6	10.2	6.8	-0.6	-1.2	210
9:00	16.0	10.2	15.6	11.8	9.6	7.1	-1.0	-1.4	210
10:00	16.2	10.8	15.8	10.6	9.4	5.4	-1.4	-1.8	210
11:00	16.0	10.6	15.2	10.8	11.2	8.2	-1.2	-2.2	210
Midnight	13.8	7.4	13.6	9.4	13.0	8.4	-2.2	-2.8	3
1:00 am	13.8	7.2	13.8	9.2	13.6	7.4	-1.4	-2.4	3
2:00	14.0	7.8	13.7	9.1	13.4	8.6	-1.6	-2.2	3
3:00	13.4	9.0	13.6	8.8	12.6	7.6	-2.6	-3.0	3
4:00	13.4	10.2	13.6	9.0	12.6	8.4	-3.2	-3.3	3
5:00	13.4	9.4	13.4	9.6	12.4	8.4	-3.8	-3.8	3
6:00	13.8	9.0	13.6	9.4	13.2	9.8	-4.0	-4.4	3
7:00	13.4	8.6	13.2	9.2	13.0	8.2	-4.0	-4.2	4
8:00	13.8	9.0	13.2	9.4	13.0	8.2	-3.8	-3.8	4
9:00	13.8	9.4	13.2	8.6	12.8	8.0	-1.0	-1.6	24
10:00	14.6	8.6	13.6	9.4	7.8	6.4	0.0	-0.4	24
11:00	13.6	7.2	13.8	9.6	11.8	9.8	0.8	-0.2	24
Noon	13.8	8.0	13.4	8.2	11.8	9.6	1.2	0.2	2
1:00 pm	14.0	8.2	13.8	9.6	12.4	11.0	1.4	0.0	2
2:00	13.8	8.2	13.2	9.2	11.6	7.8	2.2	0.4	69
3:00	13.8	8.2	13.0	9.0	12.4	10.6	3.0	0.4	69
4:00	14.2	8.2	13.4	8.2	12.6	10.2	2.4	0.6	73
5:00	14.2	8.2	13.2	8.6	13.2	11.0	2.0	-0.4	68
6:00	12.8	7.8	12.8	7.4	12.2	7.9	1.4	-0.6	7
7:00	13.4	7.8	12.8	7.2	12.2	8.0	1.4	-0.4	14
8:00	15.4	9.4	14.6	8.8	12.4	8.0	1.2	0.2	220

Relative Humidity Calculations

Workers Club   Summer

Time		SITES			
		1	2	3	4
		RH%	RH%	RH%	RH%
8:00	pm	83.0	85.9	89.0	91.7
9:00		87.0	85.7	90.7	92.8
10:00		86.9	85.7	89.2	94.6
11:00		89.9	89.9	91.6	95.7
Midnight		91.7	89.9	92.0	94.6
1:00	am	93.2	90.6	92.0	95.0
2:00		92.5	89.9	93.1	94.6
3:00		92.5	89.9	91.6	94.2
4:00		90.6	90.6	92.0	95.7
5:00		90.3	90.6	91.3	95.3
6:00		90.6	89.9	91.6	93.9
7:00		90.3	89.2	93.1	93.2
8:00		90.7	90.6	89.5	89.4
9:00		89.7	91.4	89.2	84.9
10:00		89.3	87.9	89.2	81.4
11:00		90.7	89.2	89.2	77.2
Noon		91.4	90.3	89.2	80.8
1:00	pm	90.7	90.3	89.2	76.4
2:00		89.5	89.5	91.8	73.6
3:00		88.5	88.5	91.8	79.5
4:00		87.7	94.4	98.8	83.0
5:00		88.3	81.5	86.7	94.1
6:00		82.9	82.5	87.2	89.1
7:00		82.9	82.9	74.3	90.1
8:00		87.0	87.1	74.0	86.7

Relative Humidity Calculations

Workers Club   Winter

Time		SITES			
		1	2	3	4
		RH%	RH%	RH%	RH%
8:00	pm	51.1	70.4	68.2	91.2
9:00		55.1	69.4	75.7	93.5
10:00		58.3	59.1	62.1	94.2
11:00		57.7	64.5	72.4	85.4
Midnight		48.6	64.8	60.8	88.9
1:00	am	47.0	61.6	49.9	85.2
2:00		50.1	61.5	59.5	90.8
3:00		55.4	60.1	57.4	93.9
4:00		72.2	61.8	63.9	140.6
5:00		66.0	67.3	65.1	100.0
6:00		60.4	64.8	70.7	109.4
7:00		59.5	65.8	59.1	120.0
8:00		60.4	67.5	59.1	134.6
9:00		63.3	61.0	59.3	91.1
10:00		57.0	64.8	85.5	93.8
11:00		42.8	64.6	81.5	84.3
Noon		54.3	56.6	79.6	86.8
1:00	pm	54.2	64.6	87.2	82.0
2:00		52.8	65.8	66.1	77.7
3:00		54.2	65.6	83.3	68.7
4:00		54.2	56.6	78.6	77.2
5:00		51.8	61.0	80.8	79.6
6:00		58.0	54.7	62.6	89.1
7:00		53.7	53.0	63.5	86.9
8:00		53.3	53.9	62.0	86.8

Diurnal Temperature Measurements in Shanghai

Restaurant   **Summer**
July 31 - Aug 1, 1985

Degrees in Centigrade

Time	SITES								NOTES
	1		**2**		**3**		**4**		
	Dry	Wet	Dry	Wet	Dry	Wet	Dry	Wet	
8:00 pm	28.4	26.6	28.2	26.4	27.0	26.2	26.4	25.9	No people in 1 & 2, No AC
9:00	28.2	26.8	28.2	26.4	28.6	27.2	26.0	25.6	
10:00	28.2	27.0	28.2	26.2	27.8	26.7	26.2	25.8	
11:00	28.2	26.4	28.0	25.8	28.0	26.4	26.0	25.4	
Midnight	28.0	26.1	27.7	25.8	27.0	26.0	26.1	25.4	
1:00 am	28.0	26.0	27.6	25.6	27.2	25.8	26.6	25.6	
2:00	28.0	25.8	27.4	25.4	27.0	25.8	26.2	25.6	
3:00	27.8	25.9	27.4	25.4	26.9	25.8	26.0	25.4	
4:00	27.4	25.4	26.6	25.0	26.4	25.4	25.6	25.0	
5:00	27.4	25.6	26.4	24.8	26.2	25.2	25.4	24.8	
6:00	27.4	25.4	26.8	25.0	26.2	25.2	25.2	24.8	
7:00	27.4	25.4	27.0	25.0	26.2	25.2	25.6	25.0	
8:00	27.4	25.5	26.8	25.0	26.2	25.2	25.6	25.0	
9:00	27.2	25.4	26.6	24.8	26.2	25.2	25.2	24.8	
10:00	27.8	26.0	27.6	25.8	27.4	25.4	25.4	24.8	Full of people
11:00	25.4	21.8	26.2	22.0	26.6	25.0	25.8	25.0	Some people, AC
Noon	25.6	22.2	26.2	23.4	26.8	25.4	25.8	25.0	Some in 1&2, many in 3
1:00 pm	25.2	21.2	25.8	22.2	27.0	25.6	25.9	25.2	Full of people
2:00	28.1	26.2	27.6	25.8	26.6	25.8	25.3	25.1	No fan
3:00	29.0	27.0	27.0	26.4	27.4	26.2	27.4	26.2	Some people in 1
4:00	28.8	26.8	28.2	26.4	28.0	26.6	27.4	26.0	
5:00	25.8	22.4	26.0	23.0	28.4	25.8	27.6	26.0	
6:00	26.2	22.4	26.4	23.2	27.6	25.6	26.2	25.4	
7:00	26.8	23.2	27.6	24.0	27.8	25.8	26.6	25.4	
8:00	27.8	26.4	29.0	27.4	28.9	26.4	27.6	25.2	Full of people in 2, no rain

Rainy with strong winds in site 4, almost the entire time.

Diurnal Temperature Measurements in Shanghai

Restaurant

Winter
Dec 26-27,1984

Degrees in Centigrade

| Time | SITES | | | | | | | | No. of Persons | | | |
| | 1 | | 2 | | 3 | | 4 | | Sites | | | |
	Dry	Wet	Dry	Wet	Dry	Wet	Dry	Wet	1	2	3	
8:00 pm	15.6	8.6	13.8	12.0	10.7	9.5	1.4	0.4			30	
9:00	16.4	12.6	14.8	10.8	11.4	10.0	1.0	0.6			100	
10:00	16.4	11.6	14.2	9.8	9.6	8.0	0.4	-0.1				
11:00	15.4	9.8	14.2	9.4	8.4	5.4	0.2	-0.4				
Midnight	15.8	10.6	13.6	9.2	8.2	6.6	0.4	-1.0				
1:00 am	15.4	10.2	13.8	10.8	6.6	5.2	-0.2	-0.6				
2:00	15.6	9.8	13.6	8.8	6.4	4.8	0.4	-0.4				
3:00	15.4	9.8	13.8	8.6	6.2	4.8	-1.2	-1.6				
4:00	15.6	9.8	13.6	8.4	5.6	4.4	-0.4	-0.8				
5:00	15.4	9.8	14.8	10.4	5.0	4.4	-1.0	-1.4				
6:00	14.6	8.8	13.6	8.6	5.0	4.4	-1.8	-1.4				
7:00	14.6	9.6	13.2	8.6	7.2	6.0	-1.8	-1.8	1	1	56	
8:00	14.8	9.4	13.2	8.6	8.8	7.4	-1.2	-1.2	3	1	77	
9:00	15.5	10.6	13.8	9.6	9.8	7.6	0.3	-0.2	7	2	95	
10:00	15.2	10.2	14.2	10.8	8.4	7.0	1.2	-0.2	3	3	16	
11:00	19.2	16.0	15.0	11.2	9.2	7.5	1.2	0.8	126	9	78	
Noon	16.6	15.2	18.4	15.0	11.2	9.2	2.6	1.4	165	58	150	
1:00 pm	16.8	14.2	16.2	13.2	12.4	10.2	3.6	2.2	65	10	140	
2:00	16.6	13.8	15.8	12.6	8.6	7.0	3.2	1.6	4	4	23	
3:00	15.6	11.0	15.2	10.8	9.2	7.4	3.4	2.2	1	6	90	
4:00	15.6	11.2	14.8	10.6	10.6	8.4	2.8	2.2	4	2	90	
5:00	16.4	12.2	15.2	10.8	9.2	7.4	2.6	1.2	65	5	75	
6:00	18.6	15.2	18.0	15.2	12.2	11.2	2.4	1.2	185	43	190	
7:00	18.6	15.2	17.8	15.0	11.4	10.0	2.0	1.0	185	41	190	
8:00	16.6	12.8	15.8	12.4	10.2	9.4	1.6	0.4	4	6	52	

Relative Humidity Calculations

Restaurant   **Summer**

Time	SITES			
	1	**2**	**3**	**4**
	RH%	RH%	RH%	RH%
8:00 pm	87.9	88.2	94.2	96.5
9:00	90.7	88.2	90.7	96.8
10:00	92.1	86.8	92.4	97.2
11:00	88.2	85.3	89.2	95.7
Midnight	87.1	87.4	93.1	95.3
1:00 am	86.7	86.6	90.5	93.0
2:00	85.3	86.6	91.6	95.7
3:00	87.4	86.6	92.3	95.7
4:00	86.6	89.3	93.0	96.0
5:00	87.7	88.9	93.0	95.6
6:00	86.6	87.9	93.0	97.2
7:00	86.6	86.5	93.0	96.0
8:00	87.3	87.9	93.0	96.0
9:00	88.0	87.9	93.0	97.2
10:00	88.1	88.1	86.6	95.6
11:00	75.9	72.8	89.3	94.5
Noon	77.3	81.4	90.5	94.5
1:00 pm	73.4	76.0	90.1	94.9
2:00	87.5	88.1	94.6	98.4
3:00	86.9	95.7	91.7	91.7
4:00	86.9	88.2	90.3	90.6
5:00	77.4	79.9	83.0	89.5
6:00	75.2	78.7	86.6	94.5
7:00	76.4	77.1	86.7	91.9
8:00	90.6	89.4	83.8	84.2

Relative Humidity Calculations

Restaurant   **Winter**

Time		SITES			
		1	**2**	**3**	**4**
		RH%	RH%	RH%	RH%
8:00	pm	46.7	84.3	89.7	86.9
9:00		69.6	67.1	86.9	94.0
10:00		62.4	63.7	84.6	93.5
11:00		56.0	60.7	70.1	91.7
Midnight		59.1	63.1	83.4	81.5
1:00	am	58.7	74.2	74.5	94.4
2:00		55.0	60.1	82.5	88.9
3:00		55.0	57.0	84.7	94.2
4:00		55.0	57.2	86.8	94.4
5:00		56.0	64.2	92.9	93.5
6:00		53.9	58.5	92.9	100.0
7:00		60.3	61.0	87.5	100.0
8:00		56.9	61.0	85.9	100.0
9:00		60.8	64.6	78.4	93.3
10:00		60.1	71.4	85.7	94.7
11:00		76.0	68.6	83.4	108.5
Noon		88.4	74.0	81.2	85.4
1:00	pm	78.9	75.6	79.9	83.3
2:00		77.5	73.7	84.1	80.5
3:00		63.6	64.5	82.3	85.2
4:00		64.9	65.4	79.4	92.3
5:00		66.7	64.5	82.3	82.7
6:00		74.1	77.8	90.7	84.6
7:00		74.1	78.1	86.9	87.2
8:00		70.1	72.5	92.3	84.9

Notes

INTRODUCTION

1. Jin Oubu, "Non-residential Earth Architecture in China," *Proceedings of the International Symposium on Earth Architecture, 1–4 November 1985, Beijing* (Beijing: Architectural Society of China, 1985), 166–69.

CHAPTER 1. ANCIENT AND VERNACULAR PRACTICE

1. Deng Qisheng, "Traditional Measures of Moistureproof in Raw Soil Architecture in China," *Proceedings of the International Symposium on Earth Architecture, 1–4 November 1985* (Beijing: Architectural Society of China, 1985), 68.

2. *Scenic Spots of Shaanxi Province: Qianling Tomb* (Xi'an: Future Publishing House, 1987?).

3. Jin Shixu, *The Ming Tombs* ([Beijing:] People's Fine Arts Publishing House, n.d.), 10–14.

4. Ibid., 14–18.

5. Deng Qisheng, "Traditional Measures," 68.

6. Zhu Keshan, "The Upsurge in China's Use of Underground Space," *Underground Space* 7 (1982): 3.

7. See Florence V. Dunkel, "Underground and Earth-sheltered Food Storage: Historical, Geographic, and Economic Considerations," *Underground Space* 9 (1985): 310; and Ronald Raetzman and Suzanne Wadsworth, "Atrium and Courtyard Houses: Forms Expressive Chinese Social Organization," *Underground Space* 7 (1982): 14.

8. Zhu Keshan and Xu Sishu, "A Promising Solution to Surface Congestion: Using the Underground," *Underground Space* 6 (1981): 97.

9. Bertil Lundstrom, "Demand and Technical Requirements for Food Storage in Developing Countries," *Underground Space* 7 (1983): 254.

10. Ibid., 255.

11. Cletus T. Asanga and Robert B. Mills, "Changes in Environment, Grain Quality, and Insect Populations in Pearl Millet Stored in Underground Pits," *Underground Space* 9 (1985): 316.

12. Yu Fuwei and He Guanbao, *Hanjia Storehouse in the East Capital of the Sui and Tang Dynasties* (Beijing: Cultural Relics Publisher, 1982), 28. (In Chinese.)

13. Raymond Sterling, Charles Fairhurst, Magnus Bergman, and John Carmody (interview), "China Tour Initiates Information Exchange on Underground Applications." *Underground Space* 6 (1982): 321.

14. Yuan Chiming, *Underground Grain Storage* (Beijing: China Building Industry Press, 1979), 3. (In Chinese.)

15. Yu Fuwei and He Guanbao, *Hanjia Storehouse*, 1. Further references to this useful book are cited parenthetically in the text.

CHAPTER 2. CONTEMPORARY DESIGN

1. Yuan Chiming, *Underground Grain Storage*, 6.

2. Ibid., 2.

3. Ibid., 7.

4. Huo Yan, "Cave Dwelling and Human Health," *Proceedings of the International Symposium on Earth Architecture, 1–4 November 1985, Beijing* (Beijing: Architectural Society of China, 1985), 140.

5. Dunkel, "Underground and Earth-sheltered Food Storage," 311. See also Lundstrom, "Demand and Technical Requirements for Food Storage in Developing Countries," 251–56.

6. John Carmody and Douglas Derr, "The Use of Underground Space in the People's Republic of China." *Underground Space* 7 (1982): 11 and 14.

7. Chiming, *Underground Grain Storage*, 1.

8. Underground Planning and Design Committee, ed., *Planning and Design of Underground Structures: Essays* (Beijing?: Chinese Architectural Printing Company, 1981), 121. (In Chinese.)

9. Ibid., 121–22.

10. Chiming, *Underground Grain Storage*, 1.

11. Ibid., 12.

12. For more detailed information, see ibid., 70–80.

13. Ibid., 2.

14. Xu Si Shu, "Development and Utilization of Underground Space for Public Entertainment and Cultural Activities in China," in *Proceedings: Advances in Geotectural Design; Second International Earth-sheltered Buildings Conference, Minneapolis, 1986*, ed. L. L. Boyer and R. L. Sterling (College Station: Department of Architecture, College of Architectural and Environmental Design, Texas A & M University, 1986), 301.

15. Ibid.

16. Ibid.

17. Zhu Keshan and Xu Si Shu, "A Promising Solution," 96.

18. Xu Si Shu, "Exploration into the Utilization of Belowground Space in Cities," *Architectural Journal*, no. 11 (1982): 37. (In Chinese.)

19. Zhu Keshan and Xu Si Shu, "A Promising Solution," 96.

20. Ibid.

21. Zhu Keshan and Xu Si Shu, *The Utilization of Underground Space in Chongqing* (Chongqing: Chongqing Institute of Architecture and Engineering, 1981), 2–3, (in Chinese) and Zhu Keshan and Xu Si Shu, "A Promising Solution," 96–97.

22. Zhu Keshan and Xu Si Shu, *The Utilization of Underground Space in Chongqing*, 2–3.

23. Zhu Keshan and Xu Si Shu, "A Promising Solution," 99, idem, *The Utilization of Underground Space in Chongqing*, 6–7.

24. Mushrooms are also raised below-ground commercially at the Pennsylvania State University and in Southeastern Pennsylvania.

25. Xu Si Shu, "Development and Utilization of Underground Space for Public Entertainment," 304.

26. Zhu Keshan and Xu Si Shu, *The Utilization of Underground Space in Chongqing*, 3–4.

27. Ibid., 3–5.

28. Ibid., 5.

29. Ibid.

30. Ibid., 5–6.

31. Beijing City Office of Air Defense, "The Use of Air Raid Shelters in Beijing." *Architectural Journal*, no. 11 (1982): 40–41 (in Chinese), and "Glimpse into the Underground City of Beijing." *Beijing Daily News (Beijing)*, 21 December 1983 (In Chinese.)

32. "Glimpse into the Underground City of Beijing."

33. Tung Lin-hsu and Jing H., "Developing Underground Shopping Space in the Qianmen Business District of Beijing," in *Proceedings: Advances in Geotectural Design; Second International Earth-sheltered Buildings Conference, Minneapolis, 1986*, ed. L. L. Boyer and R. L. Sterling (College Station: Department of Architecture, College of Architectural and Environmental Design, Texas A & M University, 1986), 295–300.

34. S. Thomas Freeman, Richard Hamburger, Dennis J. Lachel et al., "Tunneling in the People's Republic of China," *Underground Space* 7 (1982): 25.

35. Xu Si Shu, "Development and Utilization of Underground Space for Public Entertainment," 305.

36. Hou Xue-yuan and Su Y., "Urban Underground Space Environment and Human Performance," in *Proceedings: Advances in Geotectural Design: Second International Earth-sheltered Buildings Conference, Minneapolis, 1986*, ed. L. L. Boyer and R. L. Sterling (College Station: Department of Architecture, College of Architectural and Environmental Design, Texas A & M University, 1986), 308.

37. Xu Si Shu, "Development and Utilization of Underground Space for Public Entertainment," 304–6.

38. Freeman, Richard Hamburger, Dennis J. Lachel et al., "Tunneling," 24.

39. Hou Xue-yuan and Su Y., "Urban Underground Space Environment and Human Performance," 308.

40. Eugene Wukasch, "Underground Population Defense Structures in China," *Underground Space* 7 (1982): 16–20.

CHAPTER 3. THERMAL PERFORMANCE

1. *Planning and Design of Underground Structures: Essays*, 43.

2. Hou Xue-yuan and Su Y., "Urban Underground Space Environment and Human Performance," 307–8.

3. Carmody and Derr, "The Use of Underground Space in the People's Republic of China," 10.

CHAPTER 4. CONCLUSION

1. Carmody and Derr, "The Use of Underground Space in the People's Republic of China," 15.

Bibliography

Asanga, Cletus T., and Robert Mills. "Changes in Environment, Grain Quality, and Insect Populations in Pearl Millet Stored in Underground Pits." *Underground Space* 9 (1985): 316–21.

Banks, H. J. "Effects of Controlled Atmosphere Storage on Grain Quality: A Review." *Food Technology in Australia* 33 (1981): 335–40.

Banks. H. J., and P. C. Annis. "Experimental and Commercial Modified Atmosphere Treatment of Stored Grain in Australia." In *Controlled Atmosphere Storage of Grains, an International Symposium Held 12–15 May 1980 at Castelgandolfo (Rome), Italy,* edited by J. Shevbal, 207–24. Amsterdam: Elsevier, 1980.

———. "Suggested Procedures for Controlled Atmosphere Storage of Dry Grain." *CSIRO Australian Division of Entomology. Technical Paper No. 13.* Australia: CSIRO Australian Division of Entomology.

Barker, M. B., and Birger Jansson. "Cities of the Future and Planning for Subsurface Utilization." *Underground Space* 7 (1982): 82–85.

Beijing City Office of Air Defense. "The Use of Air Raid Shelters in Beijing." *Architectural Journal,* no. 11 (1982): 40–41. (In Chinese.)

Burrell, N. J. "Effect of Airtight Storage on Insect Pests of Stored Products." In *Controlled Atmosphere Storage of Grains, an International Symposium Held 12–15 May 1980 at Castelgandolfo (Rome), Italy,* edited by J. Shevbal, 55–62. Amsterdam: Elsevier, 1980.

Carmody, John, and Douglas Derr. "The Use of Underground Space in the People's Republic of China." *Underground Space* 7 (1982): 7–15.

Champ, B. R., and J. B. McCabe. "Storage of Grain in Earth-covered Bunkers." In *Proceedings of the Third International Working Conference on Stored Produce Entomology. October 23–28, 1983, Manhattan, Kansas.* Manhattan: Kansas State University, 1984.

China Facts and Figures: 4,000-Year History. Beijing: Foreign Languages Press, 1982.

Deng Qisheng. "Traditional Measures of Moistureproof in Raw Soil Architecture in China." In *Proceedings of the International Symposium on Earth Architecture, 1–4 November 1985, Beijing,* 64–68. Beijing: Architectural Society of China, 1985.

Donahaye, E., S. Navarro, and M. Calderon. "Storage of Barley in an Underground Pit Sealed with Polyethylene Liner." *Journal of Stored Product Research* 3 (1967): 359–64.

Dunkel, Florence V. "Grain Storage in South China." *Cereal Foods World* 27 (1982): 409–14.

———. "Underground and Earth-Sheltered Food Storage: Historical, Geographic, and Economic Considerations." *Underground Space* 9 (1985): 310–15.

Dunkel, Florence V., Zhe Lung Pu, Chuan Liang, and Fan-yi Huang. "Insect and Fungal Response to Sorbic Acid-Treated Wheat During Storage in South China." *Journal of Economic Entomology* 75 (1982): 1083–88.

Freeman, S. Thomas, Richard Hamburger, Dennis J. Lachel et al., "Tunneling in the People's Republic of China." *Underground Space* 7 (1982): 24–30.

Gilman, G. A., and R. A. Boxall. "The Storage of Food Grain in Traditional Underground Pits." *Tropical Stored Products Information* 28 (1974): 19–38.

"Glimpse into the Underground City of Beijing." *Beijing Daily News (Beijing),* 21 December 1983. (In Chinese.)

Golany, Gideon. *Design and Thermal Performance: Below-Ground Dwellings in China.* Forthcoming, University of Delaware Press.

———. *Earth-Sheltered Dwellings in Tunisia: Ancient Lessons for Modern Design.* Newark: University of Delaware Press, 1988.

———. *Earth-Sheltered Habitat: History, Architecture, and Urban Design.* New York: Van Nostrand Reinhold Company, 1983. Also translated into Chinese and published by China Building Industry Press, Beijing, 1987.

Hall, D. W., and M. B. Hyde. "The Modern Method of Hermetic Storage." *Tropical Agriculture* (Trinidad) 31 (1954): 149–60.

Hou Xue-yuan and Su Yu. "Urban Underground Space Environment and Human Performance." In *Proceedings. Advances in Geotectural Design. Second International Earth-Sheltered Buildings Conference. Minneapolis, 1986,* edited by L. L. Boyer and R. L. Sterling, 307–15. College Station: Department of Architecture, Texas A & M University, 1986.

Huo Yan. "Cave Dwelling and Human Health." In *Proceedings of the International Symposium on Earth Architecture, 1–4 November 1985, Beijing,* 135–44. Beijing: Architectural Society of China, 1985.

Hyde, M. B. "Scientific Principles of Airtight Storage." In *Airtight Grain Storage (with Particular Reference to Hot Climates and Developing Countries).* FAO Agricultural Service Bulletin 17, 1–15. [Rome?]: Food and Agriculture Organization, 1973.

Hyde, M. B., and N. J. Burrell. "Control of Infestation in Stored Grain by Airtight Storage or by Cooling." In *Proceedings of the Fifth Insecticides and Fungicides Conference, Brighton, England, 17–20 November 1969,* 412–19. London: British Crop Bot. Council, 1969.

———. "Controlled Atmosphere Storage." *Storage of Cereal Grains and Their Products,* 443–78. St. Paul: American Association of Cereal Chemistry, 1982.

Hyde, M. B., and C. G. Daubney. "A Study of Grain Storage Fossae in Malta." *Tropical Science* 2 (1960): 115–29.

Jansson, Birger. "Planning for Subsurface Space Use in Developing Countries." *Underground Space* 7 (1983): 311–14.

Jansson, Birger, and Torbjorn Winqvist. *Planning of Subsurface Use.* Stockholm: Liber Tryck, 1977.

Jin Oubu. "Non-residential Earth Architecture in China." In *Proceedings of the International Symposium on Earth Architecture, 1–4 November 1985, Beijing,* 165–70. Beijing: Architectural Society of China, 1985.

Jin Shixu. *The Ming Tombs.* [Beijing?]: People's Fine Arts Publishing House, n.d.

Lundström, Bertil. "Demand and Technical Requirements for Food Storage in Developing Countries." *Underground Space* 7 (1983): 251–56.

Nanjing Institute of Technology, Huanan Institute of Technology and Harbin Institute of Architectural Engineering, comp. *History of Chinese Architecture.* Beijing: China Building Industry Press, 1985. (In Chinese.)

Raetzman, Ronald, and Suzanne Wadsworth. "Atrium and Courtyard Houses: Forms Expressive of Chinese Social Organization." *Underground Space* 7 (1982): 12–15.

Ramasivan, T., K. Krishnamurthy, and S. V. Pingale. "Studies on Preservation of Food Grains in Rural Storage. Part I: Rural Storage of Food Grains." *Bulletin of Grain Technology* 4 (1966): 177–94.

———. "Studies on Preservation of Food Grains in Rural Storage. Part II: Storage of Grain in Villages near Hapur." *Bulletin of Grain Technology* 6 (1966): 69–75.

Ritter, J. "Grain Storage Goes Underground at the University of Minnesota." *The Farmer,* 2 June 1984, 51.

Sigaut, F. "Significance of Underground Storage in Traditional Systems of Grain Production." In *Controlled Atmosphere Storage of Grains, an International Symposium Held from 12–15 May 1980 at Castelgandolfo (Rome), Italy,* edited by J. Shevbal, 3–13. Amsterdam: Elsevier, 1980.

Stauffer, T. "Grain, Seed, Food Storage, and Farm Machinery Tie Kansas City's Use of Underground Space to the U.S. Agricultural Midwest." In *Subsurface Space, Proceedings of Rockstore 80. Stockholm, 1980,* vol. 2. Oxford: Pergamon Press, 1980.

Sterling, Raymond L. *Delegation Journal: Underground Space Use Delegation to the People's Republic of China,* 7:257–62. Minneapolis: Underground Space Center, University of Minnesota, 1980.

Sterling, Raymond L., and S. Nelson. "Planning the Development of Underground Space." *Underground Space* 7 (1982): 86–103.

Sterling, Raymond L., Charles Fairhurst, Magnus Bergman, and John Carmody (interview). "China Tour Initiates Information Exchange on Underground Applications." *Underground Space* 6 (1982): 319–22.

———. "Underground Storage for Food." *Underground Space* 7 (1983): 257–62.

Tung Lin-hsu. *Architectural Planning and Design of Underground Buildings.* Beijing: Tsinghua University, 1981. (In Chinese.)

Tung Lin-hsu and Jing H. "Developing Underground Shopping Space in the Qianmen Business District of Beijing." In *Proceedings. Advances in Geotectural Design. Second International Earth-Sheltered Buildings Conference, Minneapolis, 1986,* edited by L. L. Boyer and R. L. Sterling, 295–300. College Station: Department of Architecture, Texas A & M University, 1986.

Underground Planning and Design Committee, ed. *Planning and Design of Underground Structures: Essays.* [Beijing?]: Chinese Architectural Printing Company, 1981. (In Chinese.)

Wukasch, Eugene. "Underground Population Defense Structures in China." *Underground Space* 7 (1982): 16–20.

Xu Si Shu. "Development and Utilization of Underground Space for Public Entertainment and Cultural Activities in China." In *Proceedings. Advances in Geotectural Design. Second International Earth-Sheltered Buildings Conference, Minneapolis, 1986,* edited by L. L. Boyer and R. L. Sterling, 301–6. College Station: Department of Architecture, Texas A & M University, 1986.

———. "Exploration into the Utilization of Below-Ground Space in Cities." *Architectural Journal,* no. 11 (1982): 37–39. (In Chinese.)

Yu Fuwei and He Guanbao. *Hanjia Storehouse in the East Capital of the Sui and Tang Dynasties.* Beijing: Cultural Relics Publisher, 1982. (In Chinese.)

Yuan Chiming. *Underground Grain Storage.* Beijing: China Building Industry Press, 1979. (In Chinese.)

Zhang Yuhuan, ed. *History and Development of Ancient Chinese Architecture,* Academia Sinica. Beijing: Science Press, 1985. (In Chinese.)

Zhu Keshan. "The Upsurge in China's Use of Underground Space." *Underground Space* 7 (1982): 3.

Zhu Keshan and Xu Si Shu. "A Promising Solution to Surface Congestion: Using the Underground." *Underground Space* 6 (1981): 96–99.

———. *The Utilization of Underground Space in Chongqing.* Chongqing: Chongqing Institute of Architecture and Engineering, 1981. (In Chinese.)

Figure Credits

All figures are the author's, except those credited otherwise below. See the bibliography for complete publishing information.

4. Courtesy of Professor Hou Xue-yuan and Mr. Su Yu of Tongji University, Shanghai.
5. Redrawn after *History of Chinese Architecture,* compiled by Nanjing Institute of Technology, Huanan Institute of Technology and Harbin Institute of Architectural Engineering, 84.
7. Ibid., 85.
8. Ibid., 86.
11. After Yu Fuwei and He Guanbao, *Hanjia Storehouse in the East Capital of the Sui and Tang Dynasties,* 21, 29.
12. Redrawn after Zhang Yuhuan, ed., *History and Development of Ancient Chinese Architecture,* 420, and Yu Fuwei and He Guanbao, *Hanjia Storehouse,* 5.
13. After Yu Fuwei and He Guanbao, *Hanjia Storehouse,* 11.
14. Ibid., 14, and Yuan Chiming, *Underground Grain Storage,* 4.
15. After Yuan Chiming, *Underground Grain Storage,* 5.
19. Ibid., 7.
21. After Underground Planning and Design Committee, ed., *Planning and Design of Underground Structures: Essays,* 124.
22. Ibid., 122.
23. After Bertil Lundström, "Demand and Technical Requirements for Food Storage in Developing Countries," 73.
24. After Yuan Chiming, *Underground Grain Storage,* 9.
25. Ibid., 56–57.
26. Ibid., 75.
27. Ibid., 77.
28. Ibid., 78–79.
29. Ibid., 58.
34. After Xu Si Shu, "Development and Utilization of Underground Space for Public Entertainment and Cultural Activities in China," 304.
35. Ibid.
41. Ibid.
42. Courtesy of Professor Hou Xue-yuan and Mr. Su Yu of Tongji University, Shanghai.
43. After Tung Lin-hsu and Jing H., "Developing Underground Shopping Space in the Qianmen Business District of Beijing," 295.
44. Ibid., 298.
45. Ibid., 297.
46. Ibid., 299.
48. Courtesy of Professor Hou Xue-yuan and Mr. Su Yu of Tongji University, Shanghai.
49. Redrawn after Xu Si Shu, "Development and Utilization of Underground Space," 305.
50. After Hou Xue-yuan and Su Yu "Urban Underground Space Environment and Human Performance," 308.
51. Ibid.
52. Courtesy of Professor Hou Xue-yuan and Mr. Su Yu of Tongji University, Shanghai.
54. Courtesy of Professor Xu Si Shu, Chongqing Institute of Architecture and Engineering, Chongqing.
55. Redrawn after Xu Si Shu, "Development and Utilization of Underground Space," 305.
56. Ibid.
57. Ibid., 306.
58. Ibid.
59. Ibid., 305.
62. After Hou Xue-yuan and Su Yu, "Urban Underground Space Environment and Human Performance," 308.
65. Courtesy of designer-engineer Mrs. Song Xio Zhr of the Yellow River Scenic Spot, Henan Province.
66. Courtesy of Professor Hou Xue-yuan and Mr. Su Yu of Tongji University, Shanghai.
67. Redrawn after Hou Xue-yuan and Su Yu, "Urban Underground Space Environment and Human Performance," 308.
70. After *Planning and Design of Underground Structures: Essays,* 14.
71. Ibid., 46.

Index